WHEN ALL BALLS DROP

WHEN ALL BALLS

D
R
O
P

THE UPSIDE OF
LOSING EVERYTHING

HEIDI SIEFKAS

When All Balls Drop: The Upside of Losing Everything

Disclaimer
This book describes the author's experience and shares opinions relating to recovering from an accident and all the changes that came along with it. Some names and details of individuals in the book have been changed to protect their identity. All the rest is a true story of a survivor.

Published by Wheatmark®
1760 East River Road, Suite 145
Tucson, Arizona 85718 USA
www.wheatmark.com

ISBN: 978-1-62787-121-1 (paperback)
ISBN: 978-1-62787-122-8 (ebook)
LCCN: 2014934707

rev201401

I dedicate this book to women who want it all: love, health, and career. May you be happy, confident, and living your dreams in spite of whatever gets in your way.

A special thanks to my clan of supporters, both family and friends near and far who come from all walks of life. You were crucial in my triumph.

Here's to looking up!

We must be willing to let go of the life we planned so as to have the life that is waiting for us.

—Joseph Campbell

Your accident wasn't a life change. The life change will be the path that you choose because of your gained perspective. You will know what you want from life, perhaps leaving the preaccident life behind totally.

—Dr. R.

We cannot tear out a single page of our life, but we can throw the whole book in the fire.

—George Sand

CONTENTS

WHEN ALL BALLS DROP

PUTTING THE PIECES TOGETHER

I AWOKE FEELING COLD IN A STARK, SQUARE HOSPITAL room. I tried to look around as I heard familiar voices. I was lying in a bed covered with a flimsy, white herringbone blanket. Both my mother and my husband were sitting to my right. I heard the beeping of a monitor and several unfamiliar voices. Why was I here? How did I get here?

A nurse with a long, blond ponytail, glasses, and blue scrubs came in and approached my bed to check my vitals and IV bag. Looking up from her clipboard, she asked, "How's your pain?"

I tried to nod, but I couldn't. My neck was in a brace. Scared, I said, "I'm okay. I think?" I looked at my mother's face. She was crying. I passed my hand over my face, which was tender and swollen. I was in a hospital gown with tubes coming out of my arms and plastic cups around my calves. Every few minutes the cups would inflate and deflate. Combined with the dissonant mixture of rhythmic beeps from my monitor, the buzzing of the overhead fluorescent lights, telephones ringing, intercom crackling, and staff talking, my already-high levels of anxiety and fear rose.

Although I do not remember the few days prior to my waking up, my mother and my husband, AJ, had been by my side continually. My mother came closer to my bed, carefully touched my hand, and said, "Heidi, you arrived at the emergency room via ambulance after being struck by a tree limb outside your apartment."

"How long have I been here?"

"Five days. I've been here for the last four days."

Confused, I asked, "AJ, did you see it happen?"

Without much expression, he said, "I didn't know it happened. A neighbor saw the limb strike you and called the police immediately."

My mother continued, "The doctor and EMTs said that only minutes after being knocked out, you were taken by the fire department to where you are now, in the ICU at St. Francis Hospital in Poughkeepsie, New York."

AJ smiled and said, "Thank goodness you're addicted to that iPhone of yours. That's how I found you. You took it with you when you left to take out the trash and go for a walk. When you didn't come back, I called. You didn't answer. Instead, a doctor did. He told me you had been struck by a tree and were in the ER."

Over the next few hours, they continued to put the pieces of the puzzle together for me. Apparently, by the time AJ had arrived at the hospital the day of the accident, I had already been admitted. The doctor who answered my phone didn't know what to say to AJ, as many tests had not yet been done. The possibilities, however, were grim:

I could be paralyzed, severely handicapped, or worse. The doctor said the tree limb had given me multiple fractures on my face, head, and—most critically—a broken cervical vertebra. The right side of my face was extremely swollen and my right eye severely bruised; thankfully, there was no damage to my eyesight. The doctor told AJ that as the staff was tearing off my clothes and preparing for scans and tests, I yelled for him in a panic. "AJ, where is he? Call him. Please, call him. He doesn't know where I am!"

The doctor told me, "He's on his way. I just spoke to your husband, AJ." Because of my outburst, the doctor sedated me to prevent further damage to my spine. I was sent through four CT scans that day before being transferred to the ICU that evening.

While I was in the ICU, AJ had to make some of the most difficult phone calls of our marriage and perhaps of his life. We had met nearly ten years before while working in a restaurant on Newbury Street in Boston, he in the kitchen and I waiting tables. He was originally from a small town in Brazil's cheese state, Minas Gerais. I was from a small town in Wisconsin, *the* cheese state. AJ was a short, green-eyed Latin version of Tiger Woods. I was not nearly as dark and had many freckles, but I was also short with calico-green eyes.

When we first met, we communicated mostly in Spanish, as his English was poor. Having returned from living abroad in Spain only months before we met, I was eager to speak Spanish, and Spanish was closer to his native Portuguese than English. So, one evening after work, I asked him out—how very forward of me. He accepted and things moved fast. We quickly moved in together, but because we were both in our early twenties and from either divorced or separated families, we waited years to marry.

In the hospital the evening of the accident and faced with the need to contact my mother in Massachusetts and my father in Florida, AJ hesitated. Although he knew both of my parents well, he dreaded calling. What husband wants to say what no parent ever wants to hear—that an accident had happened on his watch?

My mother, only three hours away, gathered her things and arrived the next day. My father talked to AJ and then to the doctor, who could explain my condition in detail without AJ's thick Brazilian accent. He would stay in Florida for an update. Then AJ called my employer's office after hours to inform the company about my accident. He explained that although I had planned to return to the office in Fort Lauderdale, Florida, after working remotely in upstate New York, I would be unable to return as quickly as the next week.

Although I didn't remember any of these days, apparently I had used my beloved iPhone to update Facebook, write e-mails, talk to my father, and text childhood friends.

Via Twitter@HeidiSiefkas29 Sep 09
had a tree accident in NY this wknd, i'll be in the hospital recovering for a few weeks until the end of October. i'm not a good patient.

That shows I was convinced I was the same one-woman show as before, juggling a successful career as a globetrotting VP of marketing and public relations in the travel industry, being happily married to an aspiring Brazilian chef, owning a home in Florida, and actively hiking, traveling, running, and adventuring in my free time. I wasn't going to let head trauma, a broken neck, or heavy sedatives get in the way!

Heck, I'd been a highly competitive overachiever since birth, probably stemming from being an only child. Convinced I was a sort-of super woman, I had been on autopilot.

MY FIRST VISITORS

LATER THAT DAY AFTER FADING OUT, I AWOKE TO SEVERAL faces, but I vaguely recognized only one: Gary, the brother of my mom's husband, Frank, from New York.

I hadn't seen Gary since my mom and Frank's wedding fifteen years before. I had taught him to play "Chopsticks" on my mother's baby grand. The other visitors were two of AJ's classmates from the Culinary Institute of America, dressed in checkered chef pants and white personalized coats.

As my mother reintroduced me to Gary, I lifted my hand, pretending to play the piano with two fingers. "Yeah, I remember."

Gary responded jokingly, "You bet. I've been practicing." As I drifted in and out, they continued talking. AJ tried to introduce his friends, but I certainly wasn't in the mood to chitchat, being bruised, drugged, and dressed in a hospital gown. I had a good excuse to not socialize, or even to be a little rude.

That evening, my mother and the nurses continued to stress the severity of my situation, but I took it all lightly. Would Superwoman take a broken neck and neurosurgery lightly? Perhaps I either didn't understand my situation or couldn't comprehend it because of brain damage—or because of denial.

In preparation for my surgery the following morning, I ate and drank very little. I had no appetite anyway. Before my mother and AJ left, I asked, "I'm freezing in this gown. Can you bring me some clothes?" That night spent alone did not go well. After vomiting all over myself, I was covered from head to toe in puke colored purple by the only thing that tasted good, cranberry juice. After the nurse changed my gown, I spent the rest of the night with little sleep and in excruciating pain. The constant yet off-key beeps and buzzes from the many machines were strangely comforting. They kept me company.

In the morning, I would have been delighted to see *anyone* walk through the door but was especially grateful to greet my first visitor, the anesthesiologist. He put me out of my misery by the time he counted ten, nine, eight…

The next thing I knew, I awoke with my mother by my side.

"Did they do it already? Am I okay?"

"Yes, Dr. Z said he repaired the broken bone with netting and steel. You need to rest now."

Groggy but feisty, I declared, "I want out of here!" However, after hanging out in the recovery room, I had to go back to the ICU.

Although I remember my mother sitting with me in the recovery room, I don't remember my doctor's visit or conversation that afternoon. I was heavily drugged and coming out of anesthesia. However, from my mother's accounts, the doctor told me, "You are very lucky to be alive."

He also said a man would be fitting me for a new brace that day. It was imperative I wear the brace to make my neck, back, and torso immobile. That would aid in the fusion of my cervical vertebra. "Good news. You will be transferred out of the ICU to another floor, a normal floor, once you have the new brace."

I was happy to hear I would be moved. I *wanted* to progress. Moving to another floor meant I was one step closer to returning to my life. Little did I know this hospital stay was only one stage—and a very minor stage at that—in regaining the life I knew.

Maybe it was the drugs, the head trauma, or a combination of the two, but when the man came to fit me for my brace that day, I was disgruntled. Not only did he look unprofessional with his baggy jeans complete with plumber's crack, but he also failed to bring the right-sized brace. For Christ's sake, it was my sixth day in the hospital. Even if someone needed to order a brace in the right size, the doctors would have known about it days beforehand. It could have been at the hospital by the day I needed it.

I freely expressed my disapproval. "You have had more than enough time to get me what I need as well as to dress professionally. This is beyond insulting. Call Dr. Z!" The brace man didn't call Dr. Z, but the nurses did after he left. I was more than angry. At that point, getting out of the ICU was the only thing on my mind. But to make the move, I had to put my faith in this Neanderthal!

That outburst led to transferring me to the fifth floor

immediately, despite my not having the correct brace. I felt as triumphant as one can feel with a catheter, neck brace, and hospital gown. Unlike the ICU room, I had a window in my new room. It didn't have a view of the beautiful Hudson River, but I could see other hospital buildings and a tree-lined hill in the background.

This change was like leaving a Las Vegas casino; I could finally tell the time of day by looking outside. And another plus: my mother and AJ could come as early and stay as late as they wanted, even spend the night. No more ridiculously confining visitors' hours.

That evening, as if giving me a birthday present, my mother delivered a new pair of gray sweat pants and a sweatshirt. I couldn't wear the pants because of the catheter, but she carefully dressed me in the sweatshirt over my gown. What a huge improvement over being nearly naked in this chilly hospital! Then, for dinner, the nurses asked my mother to fill out my favorite soft foods on the hospital's menu. Just like when I was a kid, she checked off mashed potatoes, applesauce, and a peanut-butter-and-jelly sandwich. Yet with my adult palate and being married to a chef in training, I found that the food tasted worse than airplane fare. Plus it wasn't worth the pain to chew it, as my facial bones were still extremely sore. On top of it all, my throat was raw from the surgery and its incision.

While transitioning from morphine to pain pills, I became acquainted with the nurses on the fifth floor. Every four hours one of them would come, which meant more pain pills and a little company to break up my counting the holes in the ceiling tiles. Granted, some nurses were better than others; I noted a dramatic difference between the demeanors of the daytime nurses versus the graveyard shifters. Maybe the daytime shift conversations were all an act—"Honey, darling, sweetie, I know"—because I had visitors, witnesses to their behaviors. However, the night crew came in like ghosts: pop in, give meds, check vitals, and pop out to go back to texting or watching the TV until passing the patient baton to the relieving nurse.

Regardless of shift, not one of them exuded the compassion I expected from a nurse. Between the equipment provider with his in-your-face butt crack and the revolving door of nurses and specialists who failed to respond promptly to my call button due to gossiping or texting, I began to believe the term *health care professional* was an oxymoron.

Returning to My Roots

Passing the hours in a dazed state on the fifth floor of St. Francis Hospital in Poughkeepsie, I thought of another St. Francis Hospital. In the mid-1970s, I was born in St. Francis Hospital in La Crosse, Wisconsin, nearly three thousand miles away. Suddenly, I was given a second chance at life in a hospital with the same name as the one where I was born. What a rare coincidence!

Not having lived in Wisconsin since my undergraduate studies in Madison, perhaps I needed to revisit my roots.

My childhood home was a hobby farm in rural western Wisconsin. We lived nearly three miles outside of the small town of Galesville in Little Tamarack, a valley of dairy farms and apple orchards. Our cedar-sided two-story house and its twenty acres were nestled in the heart of the valley. A former orchard served as a pasture for our flock of sheep. Large maple, oak, and pine trees completely hid the house atop a small hill. The rest of the property was peppered with red sheds. One served as the stables for the sheep, another as my playhouse, and the largest for my mom's antique shop called The Little Red Shed.

Although one might expect a girl from rural Wisconsin to be conservative, my upbringing was quite unconventional. My parents nurtured me in what I would consider a quasi-hippie atmosphere. We didn't live in a yurt or at a commune, but we did have a VW van. My parents, both well-educated, consciously chose to live in tune with nature aligning with their liberal set of values, all without the influence of marijuana or an abundance of tie-dyed clothing. At our farm, my mother was the antique dealer, beekeeper, shepherd, weaver, and gardener. My father worked as a university professor in La Crosse and as a part-time bartender at a local tavern in Galesville.

Unlike children my age, I ate only homemade, dehydrated apple fruit wraps from our orchard or carob chips from the organic market in town for snacks. There were no pitchers of Kool-aid or boxes of nuclear orange macaroni and cheese for me. It was organic, homegrown or nothing, unless I was visiting my grandparents who had "real" treats. Without brothers, sisters, or neighborhood kids, I stuck to entertaining myself with our pets, including Caesar, an old St. Bernard, and numerous farm cats. My favorite, Vesta, was all white with two differently colored eyes.

If the house, barn, or antique shop got too small for my liking, I hid in my playhouse—a converted corn crib—or went up into the pasture. Although I loved being the center of my parents' world, they wanted to make sure I was well socialized. So I attended a preschool a couple days a week in town as well as classes at the university to get me ready for kindergarten. Nevertheless, I was tremendously shy, still hugging my parents' legs until I came out of my shell as a teenager.

With a strong German heritage and living in a similar setting to the popular book, *Heidi*, my parents had named me Heidi. I guess they thought it would be cute to have a girl named Heidi in the countryside playing alongside a flock of sheep! (Granted, in the book, Heidi's grandfather and her friend, Peter, raised goats, not sheep, but potayto patahto.)

This unusual childhood in rural Wisconsin taught me to appreciate my independence. From early on, I had been the free-spirited country girl who never lost the desire to explore.

WHERE'S EVEN AN OUNCE OF INDEPENDENCE?

ON THE DAY AFTER MY SURGERY, MOM CAME EARLY TO keep me company and watch my progress while AJ was in school. Midmorning, the head nurse came to take out my catheter. Although I feared the pain, the nurse reached under my gown and in what seemed like one gentle pull gave me back an ounce of my independence. It had been unsettling to be dependent and not feel the urge to go to the bathroom. However, this was just the tip of the iceberg as far as regaining my lost freedoms. I didn't know I would be like a child for months, dependent on doctors, family, friends, and coworkers.

Afterward, when I was told the staff physical therapist would walk me around the floor, I was fearful but also thrilled. As an active person whose wardrobe sported more athletic gear than three-piece suits or swanky club attire, I saw this as a glimmer of hope. I knew that to get discharged, I would have to be able to walk without much assistance.

My first steps were baby steps, each one tentative, slow, and unbalanced. Not surprisingly, I tired after walking the linoleum floor in only one hallway and told the physical therapist, "I need to sit. I'm dizzy and scared."

The therapist eased me to a nearby chair and said, "You're doing a great job. Slow and steady wins the race, right?" Although it was a compliment, I didn't feel victorious. For someone who had climbed alone to a height exceeding three thousand feet in the Catskills and to the top of a fire tower the day before the accident, ironically, I had to be awfully cautious of steps on the level hospital floor.

However, on that first walk, I did look into the patient rooms of those who couldn't walk. Despite my condition, I felt lucky. I saw them hooked up to multiple beeping and wheezing machines. Many had no family members or friends by their sides. They lay alone in dark rooms with flavorless meals and water pitchers atop their trays while their TVs played the last channel a nurse had selected.

After an entire week in the hospital, the following day was like a coming-of-age event. I was set for two biggies: a bath and a bowel movement. The head nurse who had removed the catheter the day before said, "Sweetie, you have to go number two once before you can be discharged." Before placing a measuring pan in the commode, she held it in my line of sight, saying, "This is to monitor your progress."

I looked at the container, which looked like a large upside down hat, and then at her with a skeptical grimace and asked, "Can you bring me some apple pie?" I felt like I was betraying my mom's Cortland apple variety, but I knew I hadn't eaten enough to poop. And I wanted out badly. So she said, "Sure." Under normal circumstances, I would have asked for cheddar cheese on top, but I didn't, not wanting to get more plugged up than I already was. I loved cheese, but not that much!

Then she brought out a washing pan with warm, soapy water and a washcloth. Time for my first sponge bath. I had envisioned a sponge bath much differently in my fantasies—not with a random nurse or in a hospital bed but with a sexy partner and the *Dirty Dancing* soundtrack playing, dozens of candles lit, and even a bottle of champagne.

She sponged my legs, arms, stomach, and back while I stayed in bed. I was disappointed she didn't wash my hair, which was starting to look ratty. After eight days in the hospital, I appeared as if I was prepping myself for dreadlocks.

I asked the nurse, "Can you wash this mop?"

"Because of your brace, I can't wash your hair, but I might have something that will do the trick. It's like a semiwash."

She returned with a Comfort Cap, a plastic shower cap with a liner. She microwaved it to activate the shampoo and conditioner in the liner, and then my mother put the plastic cap on my head and massaged it into my scalp. After she removed the cap and brushed my hair, I asked her, "Can I use your compact?" Although I looked as though I'd lost a bad bar fight, I gave the mirror back and said, "This is as good as it gets." And it was the truth; I looked as good as I could—bruised, swollen, in a brace, and eating bad apple pie to make me poop.

Only after that momentous event could I leave.

RELEASE ME, NOW TAKE ME BACK

ON THE NINTH DAY AT THE HOSPITAL, MY MOM LEFT EARLY in the morning to return to Boston for work. AJ and I waited together. I had already passed all the tests: I had pooped on my own, walked by myself, and given myself a sponge bath. The only thing left was getting my full immobilization brace. Once again, I was waiting for the brace man with the plumber's crack. Counting the minutes, I wondered what the bills would be from multiple days of fine dining, hospitality, and spa services at Chez St. Francis.

When the brace man arrived, I was horrified. What he brought was more like a cage than a brace—a full chest and back plate connected to a neck collar.

Like before, he arrived wearing less-than-professional attire and showed poor bedside manner. He quickly put the brace on me, gave me the instruction manual, and said, "That's it." I asked him to demonstrate putting it on one more time because I did not feel comfortable. Instead, he passed the manual over to AJ and said, "Everything's in there." How I wanted to spit on him!

Still, having this new brace meant I was free to go. The discharge nurse gave me the doctor's printout of my to-dos, which appeared to be copied from *Wikipedia*. Neither the doctor nor the nurse went over the information with me. Maybe I was expecting too much, considering I'd never broken my neck before.

AJ went down to the ground floor so he could pull the car around. As the nurse helped me into a wheelchair, I held on to it with a death grip. After all, I had moved only at a very slow walk in over a week. The quick pace to get me to the elevator and the outside pick-up area frightened me as I felt every bump and crack in the floor. I presumed the nurse was rushing to sneak in a cigarette break right after she finished with me.

Although I felt grateful to get out of the hospital, I was extremely fearful getting into the car. The ride home was a little over a mile and only five minutes. However, this time we had to make a necessary stop at the pharmacy for painkillers, which meant driving on the open road. With all the curves, stops, and potholes along the way, I had to deal with more than the cracks in the hospital floor.

After multiple attempts due to the restrictions of my new brace, I got into the car. I imagine Houdini could have gotten out of one of his tricks more quickly. And I was right. The car ride to the pharmacy with its speed, bumps, and turns was too much. How I wished for one last dose of morphine so I could get back to the apartment in an altered blurred state.

In the car, I waited *forever* for AJ to get the painkillers. All

I wanted was a bed and relief. Once we arrived at our multiple-story, brick apartment building, getting into our first-
floor studio apartment was like an obstacle course. I pivoted
my way out of the car, climbed six tricky stairs, and managed
to pass through not one but three doors. I cursed the entire
way like a delusional veteran or a recently discharged sailor.

In this studio with windows facing the street, the decor
was spartan. Like most temporary college apartments, it had
a combined living and sleeping space with a bathroom and a
one-butt kitchen. AJ had lived there for the past four months
since moving up from Florida to go to culinary school.
Although it wasn't the most secure neighborhood of Poughkeepsie, a small city of about thirty thousand people, it was
the best price and distance from the school for that semester.
During my monthly visits when I worked remotely, I had
helped get the place livable by adding a small table, desk, and
futon for lounging and sleeping. But it certainly didn't have
the love or warmth of our beautiful home in Florida.

I immediately headed for the bed, a horribly uncomfortable futon that made the hospital bed look like a
luxury, five-star hotel's bed, with its built-in TV remote,
call buttons, and the ability to elevate or recline. To endure
the new, confining brace, I needed to frequently change my
position from reclined to flat to elevated. At the apartment,
I was limited to using the few pillows we had. After experi-
menting, I found the secret recipe was only one flat pillow,
as the brace didn't allow for anything higher. If I used more,
I quickly found out it created a sensation like I was hanging
myself, preventing me from sleeping or even feeling sane.

The studio apartment lacked the every-four-hour inter-
ruptions of the hospital, which was good. I needed to be

more independent—or as independently dependent as someone could be in my situation. I ate very little, slept little, and was in a lot of pain.

Strangely enough, it was when I left the hospital that the sleepless nights began. Oh how I needed the sleep to heal! However, because of my brace, I couldn't toss and turn, just quietly count sheep. I also couldn't use my go-to method of counting the holes in the ceiling tiles because my new ceiling was cheaply painted white without even the oh-so-common popcorn for texture.

Around this time, I began to experience shooting pains in my legs. Despite walking daily to keep the blood flowing, every time I got up out of the car, a chair, or my bed, a sharp pain shot up my legs to my lower back. When I was still, the pain radiated from my toes through my legs up to my lumbar area.

During these shooting spells, I'd flash back to the agony of running the 2004 Boston Marathon. I had completed that grand physical feat but just barely. After mile twenty-three—after Heartbreak Hill and approaching Brookline with Boston's Back Bay ahead—I felt like I was running on stumps. Each step traveled up through my body, bone by aching bone. But even that excruciating pain paled in comparison to what I was experiencing now. The stifling and severe agony in my legs from running the marathon lasted less than a week, but it had been more than two weeks since my surgery. And did my legs hurt!

How I suffered those first six days out of the hospital and in the studio. All I'd wanted was to get out of the hospital, but as soon as I did, I wanted to go back. The grass is always greener, right?

THE LETTER

ALONE IN THE STUDIO WHILE AJ WENT TO SCHOOL DURING the day and worked at night, I couldn't stop thinking about what I had found.

On the morning of the day before the accident, I had gone hiking in the Catskills near Woodstock and then returned to the apartment to clean up and watch a movie. However, I felt uneasy and couldn't pinpoint why. I looked around AJ's desk and then opened his computer. Suspicious, I checked his recent browsing history and logged into his e-mail. There, I saw correspondence with a former female coworker who lived in Miami. I recognized the name because, before his move to New York, she was texting him too many times for any wife, girlfriend, or partner to ignore. When we had discussed the questionable texts months before, he said, "It's nothing." I believed him then.

This time, I read conversations in which he intimately called her by the same endearing nickname as mine— *popozuda* (bootylicious in Portuguese)!

Although my stomach turned and I began to sweat, I dug deeper. A week earlier, the woman had written an English paper for him, which he had shown me with pride when I arrived from Florida. I should have known that his Porglish (Portuguese-English) hadn't improved to the level of an English 101 term paper in just weeks. Then I found the mother lode, a multiple-page letter from her to him outlining my deepest fears. It was a confession letter of their relationship—written to him but intended for me to find on his computer. What a clever other woman!

In the letter, she wrote about the beautiful beginning of their relationship in Florida one year earlier. It revealed twelve full months of lies. Relentlessly, I kept reading. She described their passionate sexual relationship and how his accounts of our sex life being dead justified their actions. I became nauseated when I read she started taking the pill after trusting his monogamy with her. Although I felt just plain stupid, I was not alone. Hello, naive other woman. He was living like a king, having his cake and eating it too—all the while unprotected with us both.

Like adding salt to my wound, she wondered why he would stay with someone who was controlling, belittling, and not making him happy. Then she confronted him about filing divorce papers as he had promised. She wrote, "You said going to school in New York and getting out of the house in Florida was your way out. Why do you keep allowing her to visit monthly—especially after I came and visited you?"

I sat in this studio apartment that I'd financed and signed a lease for and almost growled. "What balls! What an insult!" While I kept our life in Florida afloat with my career, he was chasing a dream of being a Culinary Institute of America graduate and chef. All the while, the other woman visited freely from Miami, living off a gigolo, or more accurately, me. I had provided a place for them to rendezvous with my credit and money. *I had enabled them.* And AJ had been living a double life.

Shockingly, I didn't feel sad or even hurt, necessarily. My blood was boiling and the hair on my arms was standing on end. I felt furious about being fooled by the person I had committed myself to but who did not love me in return. How could someone say he loved me and do this? Why wouldn't he just end it before hurting me to the core? How could a twenty-something win his attention over *me*? How could I have been so blind?

I immediately texted AJ at work. "Come home, NOW!"

Then I quickly began packing my necessary things into my carry-on. Meanwhile, I continued to look throughout the apartment to find other proof, although it wasn't necessary. I had plenty. Then he called from outside the kitchen at work on a break. In a downright nasty tone, I yelled, "Take a cab home!"

Of course, he didn't want to. "I can't take a cab, Heidi. I'm going to look like an ass when I have to explain to my coworkers why my wife wouldn't pick me up."

I said angrily in return, "Well, at least that would make two of us looking like asses. I know about *her*."

He paused, and I could hear him taking a drag of his menthol cigarette. Then he explained, "I was going to come clean to you tomorrow. I have emotionally betrayed you." What a cop-out that he couldn't own up to more than "emotional betrayal" after over a year of lies and infidelity.

"The cat is out of the bag, AJ. I found her letter!"

After demanding he explain himself fully, which he said he would, I agreed to pick him up after his shift. Before leaving the apartment, I researched a number for a local taxi to take me to the airport the next day. Given that letter, I wouldn't stay the full week and work remotely as I had planned.

After his shift was over and he came out to the car, I threw him the car keys. "I'm too emotional to drive with you in the car." On the drive home, he pleaded, "Heidi, we've both had a hard day. Let's just go home. We'll talk in the morning. I'll tell you everything you want to know. I promise."

That night, he slept on the floor while I tossed and turned in the futon that disgusted me. How could I lie in the same bed where they had been? Both of us feeling restless, we got up early the next morning. It was chilly and misting, a fitting backdrop for such a melodrama. He planned to drive us across the Hudson River to the Minnewaska State Park—to talk. The park is part of the Shawangunk Mountain Range where I had gone hiking a month previously. It was my favorite area to hike with its multiple day-trail hikes and beautiful vistas of lakes and waterfalls, all framed by dense forest and rugged rock formations. He'd never gone with me because he was always at school or working.

I bet he took time off for the other woman. Did he take her to *my* favorite spot?

I could have used a walk to get rid of some of my angst, but unfortunately for both of us, when we got there the park wasn't yet open. His plan B was to eat breakfast at a diner, but I was too upset to eat. After over an hour of driving with no plan C and still waiting for his explanation, I had reached my threshold.

"Tell me the truth now!" I shouted as I pounded the dashboard. He pulled over and said, "This is why I can't do it anymore."

"So that's an excuse to have an affair for over a year? Bullshit!"

We returned to the studio without a hike, breakfast, or a confession. By then, it was nearly noon. The Patriots pregame was about to begin. I couldn't stand it. With the football game on, he wouldn't talk. It was partially my fault since I'd taught him the rules of the game so he could talk sports with his colleagues. But watching football had become an all-encompassing pastime for him, and he was an avid soccer fan as well.

Knowing I couldn't stay in the apartment, I decided to take a walk. Before leaving, I took out the garbage and an empty pizza box. That's when the tree hit me—while AJ was drinking a beer and watching the Patriots game via some pirated Internet site. Somehow he must have ignored or missed the fire department sirens and lights that rescued me. However, he did call my phone after I didn't return later that afternoon. That was when the doctor answered.

By that time, I was in the ER.

No Painkillers and an Alternative

W HAT SCARED ME NOW IN THE STUDIO APARTMENT WAS having to take care of myself in this injured state. AJ would leave early in the morning for school and go on to his line cook job at night. No one was checking in on me to see if I needed pills, food, something to drink, or just company. How lonely I felt without others around—even if they were less-than-compassionate nurses or patients in pain, too. Misery sure loves company.

Adding to my marital betrayal and physical suffering were the doctor's miscalculations. My painkillers ran out before my one-week follow-up visit. In fact, they'd run out *three days before.* I called for a refill, but the office was closed, so I dialed the after-hours number. I spoke calmly to an answering service operator and politely asked for a needed refill. After contacting my doctor, she gave me the bad news. He would *not* refill my painkillers. That's when I called my mother, crying harder than ever.

After my mom calmed me down, she needed a dose of sanity, too. Furious that she couldn't help me from a distance, she picked up the phone and called a long-time friend, Jill, in Wisconsin. Jill had had a serious health scare years before.

She asked Jill, "What did you use to remedy your pain since the traditional medications didn't work?"

"I smoked pot," she answered.

Mom blew my mind with her solution, saying, "Have AJ get pot from his classmates. I'm sure he knows someone. Then I'll bake brownies. You wouldn't have to irritate the incision on your neck by smoking it."

Her suggestion was innovative for my mother, a law-abiding citizen; however, I had smoked marijuana and eaten pot brownies before. Without the advantage of my college taste testing, she didn't realize pot brownies still tasted like an herb, not the ooey gooey goodness she baked into her brownies.

Plus, there was the oh-so-very-minor detail that pot was illegal. Regardless of the popularity of medicinal use in states that had legalized it, medical marijuana wasn't legal in New York. And even if it were, I didn't think a doctor who refused to refill a prescription for a narcotic would turn over a prescription for pot.

Walkway over the Hudson

Although most physical injuries and surgeries require weekly or even daily physical therapy, mine did not—at least early on.

Dr. Z's number one concern was that the vertebra would fuse first. The physical therapy could begin after the fusion held. It would help me gain strength in the neck, shoulder, and back muscles weakened from nonuse. Until that time, the only physical activity allowed was walking. In fact, the doctor highly suggested it, which became a savior during my recovery.

At first, I was not nearly strong or brave enough to walk down the gradual Main Street hill from the apartment to the riverbank. I feared I couldn't walk without tripping, falling, or exhausting all my energies. Plus Main Street in Poughkeepsie wasn't the safest neighborhood, however close it was to the police and fire stations. Downtown Poughkeepsie was a low-income neighborhood near the train station and was filled with questionable passersby. It wasn't a place where a Caucasian woman in her early thirties wearing a full brace would want to appear vulnerable.

As an alternative, AJ offered to take me to one of my favorite local parks, the Vanderbilt Mansion, after his classes on the occasional evening he didn't have to work. I had to swallow my pride and accept help from someone who had so deeply hurt me. But coming clean to my family wasn't going to make my situation any easier and would quite possibly make it even worse. So I endured the uncomfortable five-minute ride of shame to reap the benefits of walking freely in the park—a release from my cell-like environment. It took my mind off my discomfort and our circumstances, both of which just plain sucked.

With the changing of the leaves' colors, I looked forward to these walks and taking in the bouquets of reds, burnt oranges, and brilliant yellows at the mansion. Being sedentary in an apartment isn't good for anyone's mental health. Thus, walking became my meditation, my only dose of freedom.

After a few days of walking and feeling stronger, yet still unable to go by myself, I wanted to experience a new park, the Walkway Over the Hudson. It was a former railroad bridge from the 1800s that had been converted into a pedestrian walkway crossing the river between Poughkeepsie and Highland, New York. It was Sunday of the Columbus Day weekend when AJ offered to go there with me.

With the walkway only minutes from our apartment, we drove there, parked, and started to walk arm in arm on the path. Droves of people as curious as us were trying out the new park. My aching legs moved slowly, but with each step, the pain lessened as I went into sensory overload from my surroundings. The stares at my bruised face and large neck brace made me uneasy.

However, I was not nearly as nervous as AJ. People looked at him as if he were the abusive husband who'd done the damage. Little did they know how right they were in a certain way. The looks coupled with the unpredictable movements of dogs on leashes, rollerbladers, and small children scared me almost to the point of quitting.

Step by step, after about half a mile, I made it to the river's edge and a panoramic view that was a feast for the eyes—especially compared to my hospital and apartment views. To the south, I could see the metallic FDR Bridge and an explosion of autumn's colors on the Highland hillsides across the river. To the north, I could make out the Culinary Institute of America and the Catskills in the distant foreground. How I wanted to cross that river. But the pain was too much. Turning around felt like I had failed. That day, I couldn't walk across a bridge that only weeks earlier I would have run across on a morning jaunt.

However, this was only my first attempt.

REALITY CHECK

SEVEN DAYS AFTER I WAS DISCHARGED FROM THE HOSPITAL, I was scheduled to see my neurosurgeon. With AJ at school, my mom drove from Massachusetts to take me to the appointment and support me emotionally. For the first time, she witnessed how painfully difficult it was for me to bend and pivot my rigid body into and out of a car. By design, the seat was naturally curved for the comfort of the normal passenger, the opposite of my rigid brace.

After my minor victory of getting into the passenger's seat, off we went all of two blocks down Main Street's hill to the doctor's office. In hindsight, since it was so conveniently close, I'm not sure why we didn't walk.

As we pulled into the small parking lot, she asked, "Have you seen the tree yet?"

"I don't have the courage yet."

"Did you know it's still exactly where it fell?"

A little smug, I replied, "I do. But, I've been getting

out of the car at the front door. That's why I had AJ take photos."

Earlier, in preparation for my midmorning appointment, my mom and I had written a list of questions. When could I shower? Why was I experiencing pain in my legs? Was there anything I could do to help me sleep? When could I travel long distances by car or even fly again?

We entered the building and found his office on the first floor. Turning and pulling the doorknob, I was barely able to open his damn door. Granted, I was in a weakened state, but it was one of the heaviest doors I'd ever tried to open. What ingenious planning to have a doctor's office with such a difficult door!

Dr. Z's assistant, Kim, greeted us and asked, "Can I make a copy of your insurance card?" I was sure the surgeon wouldn't have cut me without double-checking about insurance payments. Regardless, I gave her my card as I felt my remaining energy fade fast.

We waited, surrounded by others in pain but none having a black eye, swollen face, or brace like mine. Kim led us to the examining room, which had a footstool and the highest examining table I'd ever seen. Once again, a lot of thought must have gone into the design of the examining room. Since I had trouble getting into and out of a car, chair, or bed, I needed to conquer the highest step ever to be examined. Brilliant!

Dr. Z came into the office, but I didn't recognize him from the hospital. He was middle-aged, Caucasian, a little pudgy around the middle, and wearing blue scrubs. He once again told me how lucky I was and asked how I was feeling.

"I'm in tremendous pain. And you know that my pain

medication ran out three days ago. Why wouldn't you refill it?"

He apologized somewhat, saying, "Unfortunately, narcotics are not extended when the office is closed." Whatever the reason, his answer didn't satisfy me.

"So since you didn't refill my painkillers, I called your assistant about an alternative. She told me to take Extra Strength Tylenol."

He glanced at Kim in disapproval and quickly said, "No, stop taking Tylenol. Although in some cases it would be a solution, it could harm your liver." I was livid. While I was in agony, he didn't refill prescribed pain pills and his assistant instructed me incorrectly. I would later discover this was only the first in a string of inaccuracies.

Then he asked me to lie down. I slowly eased myself onto the table and logrolled my body to the middle. He checked the tightness of the brace and my arm strength, especially my hands. Then he showed my mother how she was to bathe me for the next months. What? Did he not know I was shown how to sponge bathe myself in the hospital before being discharged? How naïve I was to hope that, after this appointment, I would be able to shower. But no. Dr. Z said, "Don't take off the brace, even to wash, unless you're lying flat on a bed." My hope of showering was shot. I had to be sponge-washed on a bed for the next several months. But I didn't want to be bathed by my mother or by AJ. It's belittling. And I'm an adult, or so I thought.

After that tremendous letdown, many of our questions for Dr. Z seemed stupid. However, I couldn't let him off easily. I wanted to get rid of the pain in my legs. And I wasn't sleeping. Also, I was curious about when I'd be able to return to work.

To address my shooting pains, he asked me to point and flex my feet. Then he prescribed both an ultrasound to check for blood clots in my legs and a CT scan to monitor the swelling in my brain. These he wanted done that afternoon. He also prescribed a slight antidepressant that would help me sleep.

Almost without looking up from his prescription pad, he stated matter-of-factly, "Heidi, you will not be traveling long distances until after the bone fuses, and you're certainly not going back to work for many months."

AJ and my mother had heard this before, but I had not. He also said, "I think it would be good for your mother to take you to her home in Massachusetts since the care that AJ can give as a full-time student and cook at night will not suffice." I had convinced myself I'd be back to Florida and to work sooner. Hearing this news created a severe reality check.

I wasn't going home; I would be living with my mom again; I wouldn't shower for months. I had regressed to being a dependent child.

And the day continued to get better.

To get yet another CT scan and an ultrasound, we needed to drive across town to a different health care office and, of course, wait. But although Dr. Z's office called in the prescription, we learned that my insurance company hadn't approved the scan. In pain, recently told that my life was on hold, and about to have a full-blown, adult temper tantrum in the middle of the office, I wouldn't wait for the hourly employee to call and get approval for the CT scan. Who knew how long we would be there? I had to take matters into my own hands.

So I called my insurance company, giving the laundry list of numbers, names, and additional nonsense needed to talk to the right person. Finally, my assigned advocate, Rich, got my call. Only days before, he'd called me as a follow-up after I'd been discharged from the hospital. What a godsend. I didn't realize that patients like me who have complicated scenarios get an advocate to expedite the approval of life-necessary tests and surgeries.

I explained my case to Rich. He said that because I received four CT scans in the ER, the system flagged the fifth as questionable. However, he quickly keyed the approval for the CT scan and the ultrasound of my legs. A small win for Heidi versus health care.

After I got both scans, we waited for the official results and then drove back to Dr. Z's office. For the umpteenth time that day, we waited for the doctor to give us his verdict and another prescription, make the next appointment, and receive needed documentation for cancelling multiple flights I'd scheduled to Quebec, London, Tucson, and Nashville.

Since the CT scan looked clear enough, we received the go-ahead to travel to my mom's Massachusetts home. We also received a prescription for more pain medication. Dr. Z was careful to advise, "This will be the last time. I will not refill them because they're highly addictive."

"Believe me, if I don't need them, I will start weaning myself off. Painkillers don't make me feel in control. I like to be in control." I crossed my fingers that he did better math than the last time. After all, I would not see him for nearly six weeks. If there were any miscalculations on pain medications this time, I would have more time to marinate in my sweat and oils without the option of a good hot shower. Just to spite him, I would return smelling like a dirty backpacker just off the Appalachian Trail minus the polite cover-up of patchouli oil.

After leaving Dr. Z's, I immediately called AJ. "The doctor said it would be better if I stay with my mom in Massachusetts for the next six weeks." He knew as well as I that it was a good decision to go to Massachusetts because the studio was not a suitable place for my recovery. It had no real comforts—no TV, no pets, nada. Plus, he only slept there. Given the latest circumstances, I bet he felt relieved. I did, too.

We quickly picked up my things from the studio and said good-bye to AJ. I wasn't sad to leave either the apartment or my husband, knowing I could escape some of the emotional turmoil while receiving TLC from my mom.

Because I was in desperate need of pain medication before leaving town, we went to the pharmacy before the dreaded three-hour car ride. With my first dose of pain reliever in days, I got into the car and prepared for an uncomfortable ride. Despite my apprehension, I was pleasantly surprised; it turned out to be a leaf-peeping excursion with the fall colors emerging in some areas of the Berkshires in western Massachusetts. Thankfully, the painkillers kicked in to quiet my pain. Halfway, we did stop to walk around and get some comfort food: McDonald's fries no less. What do they do to those fries to make them taste so damn good and be so wickedly addictive?

Near nightfall, we arrived in Chelmsford, near Lowell,

Massachusetts, to my mom and Frank's home—a modest single-family house in a quiet suburban block. It was quaintly designed like a barn, originally red like her antique shop, with a large backyard.

I greeted Frank, still with his native Brooklyn accent, and their two eager pets, Meg and Kasha. I didn't waste time finding my bed, a foldout couch in the living room. It was conveniently next to the bathroom on the first floor with a TV of my own. The room certainly wasn't private, located below the stairs, next to the kitchen, and off the dining room. But it had multiple windows with views of the bird feeder, backyard, driveway, and front yard. Many of the items in the room—from art to antique furniture—came from my childhood home. However, Frank's decorating touch was also evident, with his clock collection (a.k.a. obsession) displayed throughout the entire downstairs. For the sake of my sanity, the grandfather and various cuckoo clocks were turned off during my stay.

Their living room was quickly transformed into my Road to Recovery Suite where I stayed the remainder of the fall and beginning of winter.

THE INSTINCTS
OF ANIMALS

ONE OF THE SAVING GRACES OF MUCH OF MY MASSACHU-setts alone time was having two pets in the house: Meg, an older German shepherd, and Kasha, a mature, gray-and-black tabby cat awaiting her ninth life. I had never been fond of either of the animals; I rarely petted them. However, I enjoyed having their energy around me.

During the first days, I was at my lowest point suffering from pain in my legs and taking pain pills and napping most of the day. It was obvious that Meg and Kasha were looking out for me. Each morning I received wake-up therapy from Meg who strolled by my bed and licked me before continuing to her dog dish in the kitchen and snagging any leftovers from the cat's dish, too. Kasha, since she was smaller, was able to sneak into my bed each night. I didn't even notice until morning when a cat adorned the foot of the bed. Perhaps she thought I'd be mad, but I never was. When the house was empty with both my mom and Frank at work, the meows and barks of both animals—and sometimes their flatulence—comforted me in a strange way.

However, it was not long until the first major pet tragedy occurred. Not more than a week after I arrived, Kasha wasn't eating or drinking. She had lost weight and appeared very weak. However, she still visited my bed. The vet said there was not much to do other than put her down or wait, prolonging her suffering. Until her last days, Kasha was gracious and clearly worried about me—perhaps because she also felt uncomfortable, in pain, and out of sorts.

Meg continued to visit me throughout my entire stay. Although stinky at times, she provided company for me as well as a sort of protection from the occasional house delivery or visitor. In fact, one day the doorbell rang and Meg barked. I was waiting for a package, but with my brace I could not get a good view outside. I eventually opened the door to a young Jehovah's Witness, very clean cut, probably in his teens. He introduced himself with his mother supportively standing behind him in the front yard. He tried not to react to my brace and bruising as he focused on reciting his script, but the surprised look on his face said it all. He certainly didn't expect to be greeted by a bruised, injured woman in a cage and a German shepherd guard dog.

After listening briefly, I interrupted him. "Thank you for coming. I need to rest," I said. He handed me his pamphlet, and I closed the door. Ironically, the pamphlet stated, "The end of suffering is near." How true!

Yes, the end of my suffering was near, but how near I did not know.

ERGONOMIC ADJUSTMENTS

I FIRST BECAME AWARE OF ERGONOMICALLY DESIGNED FUR-
niture or equipment five years before my accident while
working for a successful Latino entrepreneur in South
Florida. A man of discerning taste, he ordered top-of-the-
line ergonomic furniture for the entire office. Each cubicle
got an ergonomic chair with the social areas having adjust-
able tables and stools. I thought the whole idea was a bit
silly, but then again, I was in my twenties and in good
health. I could handle an uncomfortable chair if a paycheck
was involved.

At that time, I was aware of the physical problems associated with years of office work, such as back pain from
poorly designed furniture and carpal tunnel syndrome from
daily work at computers or typewriters. But I didn't truly
appreciate ergonomic design until I needed it. After living
in a world that needed to be adapted for me, I became
more in tune with its benefits.

Because of the zero range of motion in my neck, I had

limited vision. It wasn't quite tunnel vision but damn near. I couldn't work at a computer, read a book, or watch television that wasn't placed at a certain height. Because hanging items from the ceiling was not possible and I was desperate, I made my own ergonomic furniture. My traditional set-up was a TV tray with three large coffee table books stacked to make the book or laptop level with my eyes. For reading, I used a sheet music holder that kept my book open to a certain page so I wouldn't tire my arms holding the book up and open.

Knowing that both my limitations and the needed adjustments were temporary made me more patient with the situation. These conditions wouldn't be with me every day of every week of every year for the rest of my life.

All of this reminded me again how my outcome could have been so much worse.

Supported by My Clan

I quickly learned in my recovery how much you need a clan who supports you. No single person can be there for you all the time; neither can one person know the perfect thing to say or do in every situation.

Thank goodness my mother was there for me during my most crucial health scares and recovery. She treated me with the utmost TLC as a daughter and patient. However, being in her early sixties, she also needed to continue working. My father held down the fort in Florida by taking care of our house, car, mail, and yard (with its out-of-control bougainvillea), but he was so far away. And then, I had my husband who had been there for me through the early scares and walks, but he couldn't do more (or didn't want to do more) while going to school full-time and working at night. He quite appropriately took a backseat for the rest of my recovery.

But this family care wasn't quite enough. That is why I was so grateful to have a support group that came from

UPRIGHT, LOCKED POSITION

MOST TYPICALLY HEARD IN AN AIRPLANE WHEN BOARDING and landing is the phrase "upright, locked position." While I was living in a full brace (a.k.a. my cage), it had a different meaning.

The brace was officially called the Miami JTO, which sounds like a sexy sports car that might cruise South Beach's Deco Drive. However, it really wasn't anything neat or sporty, and it certainly wasn't a head turner, panty dropper, or sexy at all. Instead, the Miami JTO was a way to make my body conform to an upright, locked position. Whether I was walking, sitting in a chair, or lying down, my head, neck, back, chest, and torso were in the same position night and day for close to six months.

Believe me, maintaining this position was extremely painful.

I tried to compare the rigid, uncomfortable straight position to an airplane ride in an exit row or that dreaded last row by the lavatories where the seats don't recline at all. I had flown an international flight in one of those rows to Brazil to meet my husband's family. Both experiences proved unbearable.

During that *Meet the Parents* trip, I wasn't well-liked by AJ's mother (to say the least). To prepare for the visit, I spent the previous six months taking Brazilian Portuguese classes. Also, as my visit was around the holidays, I brought Christmas cookies. Despite my efforts, she barely spoke to me or looked me in the eye. Because I wasn't Catholic, she commented to AJ, "She's going to take you to hell." I only became privy to their conversation upon our return to the States when I asked AJ, "Did your mother say anything about me? I didn't get the feeling she liked me."

On that three-week trip, I did not meet AJ's father, as he didn't live with his wife any longer. However, I did meet all eight of AJ's sisters and brothers—girls whose names all started with *E*: Elza, Elzamar, Ezalaine, Elaine, and Edna, and boys whose names all began with *A*: Alvin, Alnin, and Almin.

Needless to say, AJ's mom was exhausted even in naming; she had brought an almost complete soccer team into the world.

If it wasn't insulting enough to be accused of being the devil's helper, early in the trip, I was stung on the nose by a hornet while looking curiously at the tropical fruit trees around their small farm. My face quickly swelled to the size of a basketball as if I'd gained thirty pounds instantly. I looked so miserable and monster-like that AJ's younger brother insisted on taking the horse and buggy into town to get me medicine from the pharmacist. There was no family car, only horse, buggy, bicycles, and a dirt bike. Given how I looked, their first impression of me wasn't good. Likewise, mine of the family wasn't pleasant either. And then I had to look forward to a return flight to Miami from Timbuktu, Brazil, in the exit row's upright, locked position. Yippee, or better said in Portuguese, *oba*!

Although my flight home from Brazil was bad, being stuck in a cage for six months was far worse. In this immobile state, I missed the small pleasures of turning my head to the side while I slept, nodding my head, reclining with pleasure in a chair or on a sofa, or even lying on my stomach. Maybe one of the plusses of my ordeal was a new awareness of my neck and spine for the rest of my life.

Most of all, I learned to appreciate the flexibility of the body—flexibility that can be taken away at the drop of a limb.

My First Therapists

WITH AN IMMENSE AMOUNT OF TIME ON MY HANDS, I HAD the opportunity to watch more daytime television shows and read more books than ever before in my life. I noticed that the overwhelming majority of them highlighted sad or strangely odd stories. Why are people drawn to personal, yet bizarrely familiar stories?

I watched everything from a nearly naked woman wrapped in a sheet confessing her love to two brothers on *Jerry Springer* to megastars telling their stories of drug addiction, domestic violence, and divorce on *Oprah*. Then on a recommendation from my friend Caris, I also read several of David Sedaris's books. He created dramatic character sketches and humorous critiques of his crazy family, his obsessions, and other self-deprecating topics.

Why did I spend so much of my time watching, reading, and enjoying these bits? With no other schedule to follow, my days would be set up around the talk show programming, ending with Oprah at 4:00 PM. Somehow, witnessing others in dark or difficult times made me more comfortable with my own circumstances. Perhaps even the nearly naked woman wrapped in a sheet and hiding a love affair with two brothers would be convinced her behavior was normal after seeing something similar on TV.

If someone else could survive an absurdly wacko situation, I gleaned hope that I could live through my hell of a mess, too.

In my case, I felt privileged to even be alive. However, my situation was far from optimal. Losing my independence, living out of a suitcase, hiding the truth about my cheating husband from my friends and family, and being unable to shower for months while wearing a brace certainly didn't make me look like the globetrotting young female executive who seemed to have it all.

Yet there was something about watching others who had gone through trying times that made my struggles less taxing and more manageable.

After a bad day from work or just a fight with your partner, take a peek at a talk show such as *Jerry Springer,* open up David Sedaris's edgy yet pee-your-pants funny books, or flip through the *National Enquirer* at the grocery store. By comparison, your day looks like a dream—or at least something that a hot bath, a phone call with a friend, or a cold beer could cure.

If you don't believe it, try this approach. Jerry, David, and Oprah were my first therapists. And I didn't have to go anywhere but my mom's foldout couch in my Road to Recovery Suite.

Halloween and a Fallen Birch Tree

●　●　•　●

On Halloween in Pelham, New Hampshire, just thirty minutes from my mom's place, a ten-year-old boy was awaiting a hayride with a group of friends. All of a sudden, a forty-mile-an-hour wind gust toppled a birch tree. It fell on top of him. Unlike me, the boy was not spared.

This freakish fatal incident happened about a month after the evil tree struck me down in Poughkeepsie. The news of the boy certainly hit home with me and just about everyone who knew my story. After hearing about this New Hampshire fatality, more family, in-laws, and colleagues than ever called both my mother and me that following week.

To view the upside, both of our stories together made others more aware of their surroundings. A high school friend messaged me, "Heidi, we are trimming our trees in the yard and watching out for tree limbs while we ride bikes." Even Frank said, "I'm catching myself looking up when I stop at a stop sign or traffic light." My boss commented, "I've told my kids to walk with caution through the neighborhood and away from trees."

Of course, some tried to use my experience to get out of chores. One of my female colleagues from Florida jokingly said to me, "I won't take out the trash anymore. It's too big of a risk." How many other females had given up taking out the trash as well? I probably had a following of upset husbands, boyfriends, and teenage boys who were tasked with that chore for life.

Not So Lucky Missing My Best Friend's Wedding

THAT FALL, I'D HAD NUMEROUS TRIPS PLANNED FOR business and pleasure. Fortunately, I was able to cancel most of the flights due to my doctor's written travel restriction.

However, I was especially hurt by having to miss one trip in particular, my friend's wedding in Arizona. The bride, Elaine, had asked me to sing a popular song called "Lucky" for her wedding. In its original version, it was a duet with Colbie Caillat and Jason Mraz, but I was going to sing it solo. I was excited and also honored to be a part of the bridal party. I had purchased the music and rehearsed since early summer. The lyrics spoke perfectly to the intimate friendship between two people and tied in well with the adventurous traveling spirits of Jay and Elaine. It was the best gift I could offer. In fact, it was something I had done earlier for Elaine's brother, Ed, as well as for one of the bridesmaids, Adriana, another intimate friend. I had learned from past wedding singer roles that it came with a definite perk: I got to be part of the wedding party but didn't have to purchase a bridesmaid dress. Hallelujah!

While her bridesmaids and family surrounded Elaine on her wedding day, I called from Massachusetts and said, "I wish you and Jay much happiness. I would love to be there. You know I'm there in spirit." She sounded so happy as she filled me in on the previous evening's rehearsal dinner, the ceremony location, and all the mutual friends and family who had arrived.

At the same time, she was eager to get the show on the road, getting her hair done, putting on her dress, and popping champagne. Elaine, Jay, and their families honored me by mentioning me in their wedding program. They explained my intended role and noted what had happened, wishing me well and promising to visit me in Florida.

Missing my friend's wedding was one of many not-so-lucky repercussions of my accident.

JUST THE TWO OF US

IT HAD BEEN ON CHRISTMAS EVE IN OUR SMALL APART-
ment outside of Boston when AJ had asked me to marry
him.

With mixed emotions, I said yes. I loved him. We had
been together for years. It would be the logical next step for
most couples, right? However, I didn't have much faith in
marriage; after all, I was an innocent bystander hurt in my
parents' divorce.

When my parents split up, I was the first of all of my
classmates to have divorced parents. This led some parents
in town to unfairly pass judgment on me because of my
parents' choice. However, karma was on my side. By my
high school years, divorce had become as common as a
stack of dominos falling, one marriage after the other. And
I wasn't the only one with baggage from a failed marriage;
AJ's parents were also separated, which only added fuel to
my doubts. Our families' combined track records didn't lean
in our favor.

Regardless, after two years of being engaged, moving to Florida, purchasing a house, surviving our first hurricane in that house, and finding the perfect beach wedding dress for a steal (only $35), it was time to take off the training wheels. We decided to take the plunge.

With two families of different cultures, Brazilian and American, and both families having their own dividing lines being separated or divorced, our wedding would have been a modern-day Latin soap opera with a midwestern twist; think Romeo and Juliet feuding on a beach with a fusion of samba and polka as background music. We would have needed mediators, translators, a priest, and a really good bartender who knew how to make a strong caipirinha, the Brazilian margarita.

So instead of subjecting ourselves to a wedding fiasco, we eloped near Fort Lauderdale on Deerfield Beach.

On the anniversary of when we'd met six years earlier, I arranged to have a solo saxophonist play "Just the Two of Us" as I walked down the beach in my white, knee-length wedding dress carrying a small bouquet of purple lilies. Wearing something borrowed, something blue, and something new, I happily approached proud AJ who wore a blue guayabera (a popular style of shirt in Latin America) and white cotton slacks.

In the presence of a justice of the peace, who just so happened to be the husband of my florist, we exchanged our vows, mine in Portuguese and his in English. That April day at sunset, we kissed after the officiant pronounced us husband and wife or *marido e mulher*. Just like that, we were married—just the two of us.

THE LAST SUPPER

Raised in a divorced family since age twelve with parents who didn't communicate much, I had taken on the tough job of mediating about expenses, travel plans, holidays, and anything that joint-custody parents could differ in opinion on. I remember separate Thanksgivings, vacations, and even graduation dinners. The year before my accident, I had asked a favor of both of my parents, knowing that someday it would come in handy.

At that time, my father had recently moved into our Florida neighborhood, only about two blocks from our house. The set-up was similar to that of the show *Home Improvement* with the neighbor, Wilson, looking over the fence. However, in our case, the person looking over the fence and coming over frequently was my dad. Needless to say, it wasn't easy for AJ to handle. Around the same time, my mother had planned her typical yearly visit around my birthday in November.

With both of my parents in Florida, I requested that we

have a family meal. The last time that occurred, I was ten. It was in Puerto Vallarta, which was my first trip of many to Mexico and our last family vacation. From what I recall, my mother spent most of the trip with Montezuma's revenge in the hotel room while my father hung out on the beach like the professional beach bum he'd always been, given his easy professor hours.

With AJ's help, we created an epicurean meal of grilled buffalo steaks, sautéed Brussels sprouts, beet salad, and bananas foster, while making sure everyone had plenty of his or her libation of choice to take off the edge. I imagine it was tense for my parents, but I felt like this could be the end of my role as mediator. For once in front of both of my parents, I relaxed and had a great time. Perhaps it meant that, when AJ and I had a child, my parents would visit in the hospital somewhat cordially. I even made a comment about that: "Thank you for agreeing to this. I asked for the dinner just in case the next time you should see each other, say at a birth of a child or in case of an accident, that you could be civil or even friendly."

Little did I know I would fall prey to an accident and would label this request either an uncanny foreshadowing or a lucky coincidence.

One Person Missing

REACHING OUT TO MY CLAN REGARDLESS OF HOW—PHONE, text, or Facebook—made me feel much better. All of it was therapeutic.

There was something about sharing my story with others—albeit the abbreviated version omitting a large painful subplot—that solidified what had happened but also what was to come. It was overwhelming yet gratifying the number of wishes that came my way, many from out-of-the-blue contacts. I gratefully received supportive e-mails, cards, flowers, and messages from all corners of the world.

Through this outreach, I realized that all of those people cared about me from afar. But I did want to see one person who had been missing: my dad. After all, I was a daddy's girl. I'd lived with him in Wisconsin after my parents divorced. Also, he and I saw each other almost daily in Florida.

So I called, asking him to come and visit me in my mom's territory. Of course, he would have preferred to see me anywhere else. Even after more than twenty years of being divorced, my parents didn't enjoy each other's company. However, I would not be in New York for another month for a doctor appointment. And I couldn't go another full month without seeing him.

When I told my mom I wanted him to visit, she said, "So, what am I, chopped liver?" She instinctively felt I was choosing him over her, but the reality was I wanted *both* of my parents around me, not only one. I didn't want to have to choose between them or have only a piece of my family.

Although it was considerable work shifting schedules, arranging tickets, and booking hotels and rental cars, my mom, her husband, my dad, and I made it happen. Early in my recovery still, I had a bruise on my face and a blood spot in my right eye. I was also still taking four painkillers a day, needing an afternoon nap, and having little appetite.

My dad had not seen me since I left for New York. He was the one who had driven me to the airport, and the next thing he knew, I was in the emergency room going through multiple CT scans and neurosurgery.

Before meeting him at the airport this time, I was apprehensive. I was not his energetic daughter of old. But when I saw him, all of my nervousness disappeared. He said, "You're my favorite daughter" as he hugged me cautiously. That was always an inside joke because I was his only daughter. But it had made me feel special as a young child and again as a dependent adult.

In some ways, it was an easy visit. He stayed at a hotel close to my mom's home and rented a car to drive us around. He accompanied me each day on my walks along the town's bike trail. The trail led to Heart Pond, which was surrounded by New England–style, gray, shingled homes with canoes and fishing boats. How wonderful to share with him the beautiful tail-end of the fall color change, which I'd previously described over the phone and sent pictures of by e-mail.

But in other ways, it wasn't an easy visit. More than anything, it was awkward for my father to come to my mother's home, especially since she had married Frank when I was still in high school. Regardless, I needed to be surrounded by all of my important people for *my* healing—and essentially for *their* healing, too.

During that week, I felt better just knowing Dad was around. It was reassuring he thought I was recovering well, having seen much improvement from the photos that AJ had sent from the hospital. During the week he stayed in Massachusetts, the bruising on my face and the spot of blood in my right eye disappeared. It was at that time I started to see the outside heal and knew the inside was doing the same.

After his visit, my father understood more about what I was feeling, what I was doing, and how I had progressed. It was helpful for him to see my cage, how the walking helped me, how the house was set up, and how limiting just sitting, lying down, or riding in a car could be.

Although hearing from my dad I was doing better felt encouraging, still, I had to prove that to two other important judges: my doctor and me!

HIPPOCRATIC OATH

DO YOU REMEMBER WHEN DOCTORS WORE BEEPERS, checked in at the hospital or office whenever the beepers went off, and actually called patients? That may have been true way back when, but it certainly wasn't at the time of my case—or at least as far as my doctor was concerned.

Remember that I ran out of painkillers just days out of the hospital? I called Dr. Z's office and was quickly directed to an answering service operator who relayed the bad news of no refill. That's when my mother came up with the creative, yet illegal, solution of pot brownies. With that operator's call, I didn't start mixing up a batch of brownies to self-medicate, but I did lose all faith in the Hippocratic Oath as taken by my doctor. Didn't he vow to do no harm? Why leave a patient in pain? Why didn't he at least call me back personally?

And that wasn't the only strike against my doctor and his bedside manner.

At the end of my first doctor's appointment, I made

my next appointment for six weeks later. It was scheduled close to both Thanksgiving and my thirty-third birthday, each extremely special to me that particular year. I anxiously waited during those weeks, each morning marking an X for progress on my Day Planner. It functioned not only as my countdown but also my journal and, due to grogginess, my "don't forget" list. I looked to my Day Planner fully anticipating a return to my life in Florida before the end of the year.

However, only days before the appointment, Kim, Dr. Z's faithful assistant, called to say he couldn't see me because of a trip to Arizona. "Dr. Z has a speaking engagement. It was unexpected, but we will need to change your appointment. Could you come the following week?"

Mortified, I had been using the date of the appointment as my beacon of light that perhaps I would return home soon. I would once again sleep in my own home instead of being an injured vagabond shuffling between Massachusetts and New York. Once again, my interests were subordinate to the personal time off or career advancement of a health care professional.

Feeling distraught, I told Kim, "I have to call you back."

Frankly, I couldn't speak to her. Crying, I needed to step outside and walk around the block. Not only were my birthday and Thanksgiving ruined, but also knowing what was going on with my recovery was postponed. When I called my mom at work to vent, she wanted to reframe the situation. "Heidi, it's only a matter of days. You can still celebrate your birthday and Thanksgiving with or without a doctor's appointment."

Regardless of her sane rebuttal, I realized I irrationally

hung on to the appointment date and my birthday as the time I'd hear news about my health and an update on when I could return home. I was crushed. I couldn't believe that I, a patient, was being passed over for a speaking engagement. So much for making *me* a priority. However, like most things with the health care system, I had to meet it on its terms.

I called back the next day and took whatever date Kim could give me. That meant getting an appointment with Dr. Z for ten days later than the original appointment. I think the schedule change was due to a legitimate speaking gig, but it helped me to joke about my misfortune by saying he was skiing in Aspen or fishing in Bermuda.

Dr. Z, you may be a wonderfully talented surgeon, for which I am thankful, but your bedside manner leaves a lot to be desired. What I needed most at the time was both surgical skills *and* follow-up.

WINE–NECTAR
OF THE GODS

I HAD BEEN A WINE LOVER SINCE LIVING IN MADRID AND traveling throughout the Iberian Peninsula in the late nineties. There, I had learned to enjoy *rioja, cava,* and *tempranillo.* As well, I gained a command of the Spanish language by immersion, which is the best and fastest way. When I returned to the States, I used my experience to teach both Spanish and English as a Foreign Language in the Boston area.

However, after a few short years, I gladly left the public school system. I quickly found out that my high school audience of one hundred fourteen-to-eighteen-year-old teens was not a captive one, regardless of whatever cartwheels, dance lessons, and cooking field trips I organized to teach more than *tú* versus *usted.*

That's when I switched from a career in education to hospitality—mostly event management, PR, communications, and sales—for restaurants both in Boston and in

Florida. I eventually left hospitality to work in travel, but before I did, I built on my wine knowledge from Spain by attending wine vendor seminars. I could taste, swirl, sniff, and parlay enough wine trivia to be dangerous in any wine circle.

Despite wanting to take away my pain, boredom, and the emotional unrest of my situation, I couldn't partake of a glass of wine or drink a toast to myself for the first two months of my recovery. The painkillers affected my liver, so it would have been too dangerous. Eventually, I started weaning myself off the painkillers for numerous reasons: lesser pain, greater appetite, and general dehydration. The latter led to many unpleasant side effects such as dry skin and habitually chapped lips, but nothing compared to the most devastating, severe constipation. I started at four pills a day for the first month out of the hospital. By the time my father visited, I had slowed from three a day to none by midmonth.

One Friday night shortly after, I experimented to see if I could enjoy red wine as I had before the accident. Affirmative!

It tasted great, but its warm, calming effects and buzz hit me with only the first glass. In a weird way, I believed that, with a glass of wine, I was gaining freedom because I was doing something I'd enjoyed before. It was yet another sign I was getting better.

So from then on, I relished wine as a part of my daily ritual. I actually had my own happy hour after spending the day with my therapists (daytime TV and books) or battling through insurance claims, bills, and bullshit paperwork.

It was always wine-thirty somewhere.

COLD CALL WITH A
CASEWORKER

AFTER I HAD BEEN OUT OF WORK AND RECOVERING FOR two months, my peers who had gone through similar long recovery periods suggested I needed to start the filing process for long-term disability sooner rather than later. I didn't want to be in that boat. What I really wanted was to go back to Florida and get back to work. However, the cold, hard truth was that my recovery was going to be much lengthier than what I'd hoped. In another month, my health insurance would end unless I filed for long-term disability. If approved, I would be allowed to continue my recovery under Cobra insurance.

If I wanted to continue to have health care, I had no choice.

After receiving the forms from human resources, calling my doctor and employer, and following up on those calls, I completed and submitted all the paperwork necessary to get the ball rolling. What a hefty package. I had to admit I'd seen graduate theses that had less paper.

Shortly after, on a Monday morning well before nine o'clock, I received a call from my long-term disability caseworker, Mandy. With all the fraud out there, it didn't surprise me I would have to jump through many hoops, and I expected some investigation on her part before the call, especially considering the number of details the insurance company required in its forms after forms after forms.

However, I must have been Mandy's first call that morning, a cold call. How appropriate! Mandy, sitting in her cubicle surrounded by other paper pushers on their headsets, didn't know anything about me, my employer, my title, where the accident took place, or the type of injuries I had. Where was all that paperwork?

The phone call wasn't a conversation or at least I didn't consider it one. She wasn't truly listening. Rather, she was typing notes and waiting for her opportunity to speak again. It was clear her questions were scripted: "What was your injury? Were you working at the time?" She was clueless *and* a bad actress. Could she have done a little homework? Could she have been more compassionate considering the topic?

After learning about my freakish accident and its severity, she asked, "What type of neck brace are you wearing?" I was so sick of describing it. Again, I pressed my inner recording and explained my cage. "The best way I can describe it is that I am in full NFL gear. I have a Miami JTO brace, which encapsulates my chest, back, and neck from my belly button to my chin and the same on the back side.

I have limited movement, can't shower, and can't drive, let alone be in one position more than fifteen minutes at a time." Coldly, she transitioned to her next question, "What were your duties and position at your employer?" This was followed up by my favorite question, "How does this make you unable to continue your responsibilities?"

I didn't know how to explain all of the intricacies, but I started to describe my executive-level position, the travel required both domestic and international, and the management of a marketing and PR team as well as contractors. To address her last question, I answered, "My job and home are located in Fort Lauderdale. I'm currently in Massachusetts under the care of my mother. I was given clearance from my doctor to travel to her home from New York where the accident occurred because my husband was unable to care for me properly in New York. I'm recovering from a broken neck with much pain and very limited abilities: no showering, no driving, no traveling long distances, especially not back home to Florida."

If that wasn't enough, I explained that because of the limits of the brace, I couldn't sit, stand, or lie in any one position for long without excruciating pain. I certainly couldn't perform six to eight hours of computer work at a desk, even with breaks. Plus, if I had to go into the office, how would I get there? I couldn't drive.

At the end of the call, she stated, "I need more information from the doctor as well as an authorization from you for obtaining your complete medical records."

She was clear in saying the records would include everything from STDs to drug dependency and general health. Honestly, at that point, I had gone through having my clothes torn off in the ER and sponge baths by my mother and random health care staff. I had nothing to hide from this woman. I was so far past the common advice you get from mothers and girlfriends to make sure you always wear clean underwear and shave your legs. I thought, "Go find a needle in the haystack of my records!"

However, the fact that I had to get a signed authorization form back to her would mean printing out an e-mailed document, signing it, and then faxing it. That would be delayed until the next day so Mom could drive me to a local fax machine or do it for me between meetings at work.

Regardless, I was told I would receive an update from Mandy within a week. If all checked out, I would receive at least a portion of my salary monthly until I was able to return to work.

However, the news was a mixed bag. I would make a percentage of my previous salary, but then I would have to pay Cobra insurance out of that. So, in essence, I was taking a pay cut back to when I was a high school teacher. I would barely be able to pay the mortgage in Florida, not taking into account all of the other life expenses: car payments, association dues, cell phone bills, Internet bills, cable, electricity, food, and more. I realized that in even the best-case scenario, I would have the rug taken out from underneath me. My good credit would plummet, not because I didn't want to pay, but because I couldn't. I felt defeated.

And I could say good-bye to financial stability.

CALLING THE COPS
ON MY BIRTHDAY

TURNING THIRTY-THREE PROVED TO BE A SPECIAL BIRTHDAY. I had survived being clobbered by a tree, luckily sparing my life but nevertheless putting it on hold.

To celebrate, AJ suggested picking me up at my mom's home and taking me to Poughkeepsie to view the tree where the accident occurred. He said he would bring me back to Massachusetts two days later for Thanksgiving. I accepted. Granted, I was leaving my mom's TLC to stay with AJ, who still hadn't come clean, but clearly I was in denial. Wasn't I supposed to celebrate my birthday with my husband?

Indeed, I was putting on a good show for all, including myself.

He picked me up on my birthday, November 24. Just before he arrived, I put on my wedding rings, which had remained in a ziplock plastic bag along with other jewelry I'd worn the day of the accident. On our ride to New York, I asked AJ about his promise to tell me the truth.

"Heidi, it's your birthday. Let's not talk about this now. I'll tell you everything when we are back in Florida together and when you are healthy."

I hesitantly agreed, but I regretted it for months. The big elephant would be in every room while he, the other woman, and I were the only ones who knew it.

After a three-hour car ride talking about his classes, exams, and work, I saw the evil tree for the first time. I had seen it before in photos, but on my birthday, it warranted an up-close-and-personal visit.

In fact, I wanted to touch it. So AJ and I walked the same route I had gone that day to take out the trash. To my dismay, the limb still graced the parking lot. My mouth dropped wide open as my eyes just stared at the monstrosity. I was more than stunned. How could anyone survive the sheer weight of a limb that size? And how is that person me?

Yes, it was considerably larger than the pictures made it appear. It was frightening to see it, feel it, and then rethink the past month and a half of recovering from what everyone told me was a miracle. Only then—after neurosurgery, numerous CT scans, and time—did I begin to comprehend the severity of everything. And confronting that damn evil tree helped.

To treat myself while AJ went to school, I took a walk along my Road to Recovery Bridge, the Walkway Over the Hudson. This time, I made it all the way across from Poughkeepsie to Highland and back. With the fall colors gone, a crisp, winter-like wind was traveling down the Hudson River from the north. I joyfully recognized that I didn't feel nearly as scared as on my first walk on the same path.

Granted, it was still exhausting to walk across the bridge, but it gave me the opportunity to conquer that physical feat—and on my birthday.

That evening, I rode up with AJ to Rhinebeck, a quaint, artistic town preserved in time with its tree-lined streets and only one intersection. That's the town where he worked evenings. I went to the independent theater across from his work and watched my first movie that wasn't on DVD or TV but on the big screen. Although delighted to do something I'd always loved, I fidgeted throughout the entire movie, wishing I was sitting in my ergonomically designed seating creations. My body ached to lie down, slow down, and get relief.

Until AJ's quitting time, I decided to enjoy a glass of red wine and my favorite crispy thin crust margarita pizza at his work. On previous visits, I'd noticed weird vibes from the staff in mannerisms and looks but more so than ever that evening. I assumed it was a general discomfort talking about the accident and brace, but perhaps they were uneasy knowing about the other woman who had also frequented the restaurant.

Still, I disregarded the looks because something else was bothering me; my father had not called. And it was my birthday. I had tried to call him a few times before entering the movie and then many times afterward. It was already seven o'clock in the evening, and I was worried. Why would he choose *this* year of all years to not call on my birthday?

I needed to bounce my thoughts and feelings off someone. So I called my mom. She agreed it was weird and suggested I should call someone to go and check on him. I had no one in Florida; my friends in the area didn't live close.

Regretfully, I had not been neighborly enough to exchange phone numbers with people nearby. In my defense, who is neighborly in Florida anyway? With such a transient population, many keep to themselves—except after a hurricane. That's when all become good friends lending or borrowing extension cords, chainsaws, and generators.

After a quick conversation with Mom, I decided to contact the local police department in Florida. So I stepped out of the restaurant to call, leaving my wine and half-eaten pizza at the counter. As I paced back and forth on the sidewalk, I knew what I'd say would seem otherworldly, but I feared that something had happened, whether a fall or a heart attack. After all, it had to be something serious enough that my father didn't call his only daughter who had nearly died.

The police station's receptionist, a woman, politely answered the phone. Following protocol, I told her my name, address, where I was, and that it wasn't an emergency. "I know this must seem strange, but my seventy-four-year-old father has not called me on my birthday. I recently was in a traumatic accident, and he and I are very close. He is living by himself in Plantation. I'm recovering up north. He would not miss calling me on any birthday, let alone this very important birthday. I have tried calling him at least seven times from this afternoon to present. He is not picking up."

I continued by giving his information, telephone number, and address. After a short wait, she said, "I have an officer available. I'll send a car over to check on your dad and the house."

Relieved and grateful, I said, "Thank you so much.

Please give me a call whenever you know something." Then I went back to the counter in the restaurant. Worried about my dad, I didn't feel like celebrating.

Within a half hour, I received a call from an unknown number in Broward County. It was an officer at my dad's home. He passed his phone to my father who said, "I'm sorry you were so concerned. I tried calling, but I didn't get you or your voice mail. I'm okay."

"You scared me. I have called you more than seven times. It's my birthday today. Especially this year, I couldn't imagine why you hadn't called."

He knew then that his phone needed to be checked. Before returning the phone to the police officer, he said, "I will call you when my phone is fixed." After the call, I was overjoyed, almost giddy. I texted my mom to let her know. Later, she admitted to saying over and over in her head that night, "Don't you dare die on her birthday."

Immediately after getting his cell phone battery replaced, my dad called me. I asked him, "Why didn't you call AJ after you hadn't reached me on my birthday various times?"

He said, "It didn't occur to me."

"Well, it should occur to you from now on, especially considering I'm recovering from a bad accident and things happen like evil trees falling."

So I went back to my pizza, which was cold, and my unfinished glass of wine. But I was no longer hungry or thirsty. I'd had enough drama for one day.

I'M THANKFUL FOR...

AFTER A QUICK VISIT IN POUGHKEEPSIE FOR MY BIRTHDAY and the start of the Thanksgiving break at his school, AJ drove me back to my mom's for a special feast. Although I had been fortunate and thankful for the life I had previously, that particular Thanksgiving had an especially sweet meaning. Not only was I alive, but the fact that I'd be able to recover and be my normal self in time was paramount.

I had never experienced a Thanksgiving like this before. Having a very small family and being blessed with good health, I knew I should never take life for granted because I had almost lost it all. I should honor my family, friends, health, wisdom, and myself not only on Thanksgiving but all year.

Despite living in a time-starved, multitasking society, people should be able to live a life that pays respect to those who helped them get where they are, to have fun being who they are with whom they love, and to never let an opportunity pass them by. That's my new belief.

I shared my gratitude with my mom, Frank, and AJ. "I'm thankful for getting to the hospital in time to save my life. I'm also grateful I was not at the hospital alone. And I'm especially thankful for the lessons this experience has taught me." Before we began to eat the massive feast my mom had prepared, I said, "Everyone must remember that it is not the house, clothes, car, or jewelry that's important. It's your health and the people you have around you. The most valuable possession you have is your health, followed closely by your relationships."

In that moment, I understood why around the world people toast with the words "to your health" or "salud." And with my newfound appetite, I planned to have two pieces of my mom's apple pie with cheddar cheese on top. I wanted to make up for insulting her expert baking skills by eating the pie in the hospital only so I could poop.

Will This Ringing in My Ears Ever Go Away?

AFTER THE BLUNT TRAUMA TO THE RIGHT SIDE OF MY head, face, and body, I expected some things might never go back to normal but would still improve over time.

I was pleased seeing the exterior bruising fade away, having my pain diminish, and continuing to receive good news from the CT scans. However, I still had ringing in my ears. In the hospital, it started out as reduced hearing on my left side. Everything seemed muted, as if my ears were clogged with water or needed to pop. It gradually changed within a few weeks. I could hear better, but what I heard was a constant ringing, almost like the static sound of a TV.

Coincidentally, I thought perhaps the ringing in my ears was a side effect of my medication. I flashed back to being a child with a fever and taking Tylenol. Sometimes after a day, I had ringing in my ears. My father explained to me, "The ringing in your ears indicates you have probably taken a little too much Tylenol. You should wait a little longer before taking more." I don't know if this is true or not, but it was certainly in my head during the process of weaning myself off of my pain meds. Perhaps I could get rid of my constipation, dry skin, general fogginess, and the ringing in my ears by eliminating the painkillers.

I had asked the doctor, "Will this ringing in my ears ever go away?" Much to my chagrin, his response was "I just saw a ninety-year-old woman who had lived through a bombing in World War II. She still has ringing in her ears; so, unfortunately, yours may never go away." Thanks for the encouragement, doc!

Even though TV, books, pets, and my friends and family kept me company during my multichaptered journey, the ringing in my ears did, too. Although at times I was lonely, I never seemed to be alone. I shared my life with static. I wished I could simply hit myself over the head like an old TV with rabbit ears and make the ringing go away.

CERVICAL SPINE INJURIES: MORE COMMON THAN YOU THINK

BEFORE MY ACCIDENT, I HAD NEVER BROKEN A BONE OR endured a major injury. I had no more than basic information about C spine injuries, knowing they occurred in horrible car crashes or from adventure sports, including our barbaric professional football game. However, I had no idea how common they were. As I went through normal daily life dressed in my Miami JTO brace, other survivors came out of the woodwork spontaneously. They'd show warm support, they'd vent, and they'd give me tips.

In fact, while I was on one of my recovery walks over the Hudson River, a gentleman sincerely wanted to tell me he'd been there, too. He encouraged me by saying, "It will pass. You will get better, but the road is lengthy." Hearing that optimism from a survivor was comforting.

Then I found out from my good friend Karol that her husband, Will, whom I had known for many years, had also had a C spine injury. It was as if I suddenly had a clandestine C spine support group. The key to joining such a group wasn't a secret handshake or hazing. In fact, you didn't get invited to the meetings or conversations until you had to wear a brace.

Although it took time, I, in turn, returned the favor of the Hudson River Valley gentleman. I saw a man in only a Miami J collar, not the full back and torso brace like mine, and said to him, "It will get better." I followed up by asking, "How are you sleeping?" His wife's look said it all. We began swapping techniques to make sleeping like a rigid board more bearable.

I don't know which of us was more comforted by our meeting—the man in the Miami J collar or me.

I'VE BEEN WAITING
FOR *THIS?*

THE SECOND DOCTOR'S APPOINTMENT HAD TO BE BETTER than the first, right?

The last time Dr. Z saw me, I was afraid, wasn't sleeping, was in pain, and was only a week out of the hospital. At that time, I had not digested the reality that I would not be going back to my former life for months. So after progressing to walking on my own, eating solid foods, slowly getting more energy, and reducing painkillers to nothing by the second appointment, two months had passed. I was back again with my mom at that Main Street Poughkeepsie medical office.

Before arriving there, my mom and I had already gone to get a CT scan, number six. We waited once again and Kim showed us to the same room, commenting on how much better I looked. I entered the room seeing the examining table and footstool with different eyes. The high table was no longer a challenge. I could easily get up there.

Regardless, I still needed to lie down and rest. I was exhausted because of the three hours in the car as well as the stress of not knowing what good or bad news I would get from Dr. Z. Nearly twenty minutes had passed before he finally joined us.

Surprisingly, he spent only five minutes with us. He had me remain lying down. After saying the CT scan had come back clean, he quickly checked the strength in my arms and the grip in both hands. It was clear he was still concerned about my motor abilities.

Like the last time, my mom and I had formulated questions.

"The brace is incredibly uncomfortable. Can I take it off while in bed to relieve pain?" He disapprovingly shook his head no. And like a bad penny, I inquired as in my first appointment, "May I shower? Perhaps in a shower chair?"

He said, "No showers. I'll see you at our next appointment in six weeks."

That was it? After waiting six weeks, riding in a car for hours, and dragging my mom with me, I was expecting to get a different response considering my situation and improved physical state, but no. It was the Jiffy Lube of neurosurgery follow-up appointments without the little reminder sticker inside your windshield. In five jiffy minutes, I faced a major roadblock. My hopes of returning to Florida to celebrate the holidays and the New Year were shattered.

After getting in the car, I asked Mom, "Why hadn't we been informed of a definite time line for my recovery? It'll be a total of twelve weeks before the next appointment!"

"Dr. Z has always said recovery will take months. I know you are upset."

I ranted. "Oh, I'm more than upset! It just isn't *right*. I could have used that information from the beginning. I thought I'd be in Florida soon." In tears, I said, "I just want to go home."

Honestly, the second appointment wasn't even worth the drive from Massachusetts to New York. I could have easily gotten a CT scan done in Massachusetts and sent it to him for the brain and spine images. He spent a grand total of five minutes with us. The six hours in the car were far too risky for the exchange of zero information on his part. He gave me no indications about my prognosis or really any positive feedback other than the results of the CT scan. What did five minutes of his bad humor cost?

I sarcastically looked forward to receiving his bill to see why we drove six hours to squeeze into his schedule. I bet it raised his revenue by hundreds of dollars. Perhaps this rescheduled second appointment paid for a couple rounds of golf in Arizona after his so-called speaking engagement.

WHEN ONE CAN'T
TRAVEL, READ

FROM THE AGE OF TEN AND MY FIRST TRIP TO PUERTO Vallarta, traveling had been a large component of my life, both personal and business travel.

Before the evil tree accident, I traveled for work for years schlepping from one travel and tourism show to the next—from Mexico City and Berlin to Vegas and London. So when people asked, "Are you traveling for business or pleasure?" I answered, "Both."

For me, it was normal to live out of a suitcase for a few weeks, many times wondering which city I was waking up in and often questioning my current time zone. However, I was traumatically taken from a jam-packed travel lifestyle to a sedentary one. This time, I was forced to live out of a suitcase—a carry-on, mind you—without the right attire for months on end. Regardless of the futon or foldout, the numerous beds I had were not nearly as comfortable as an alternative in a hotel. And, above all, being sedentary wasn't fun; it was torturous. It was a busy bee's prison; albeit I didn't have to be afraid of dropping the soap in the shower because there weren't showers either!

So with that said, I needed to travel away from my four walls without leaving. I found a considerable amount of escape through reading—everything from bestsellers to classics to lifestyle- and career-related books.

Previously, I didn't read regularly, preferring to veg with the TV oscillating between the Food Network and the Travel Channel. However, I couldn't imagine surviving my recovery without reading for hours each day. It let me break loose of my reality, keep my mind active, and learn a new way to frame my circumstances.

And from reading more, I became a better writer. Writing had always been like pulling teeth for me when I was a child in front of the Apple IIc computer in my father's den. However, after I learned a second language, my writing matured and the process became less work and more fun. It was during my daily reading time that I enjoyed traveling with writers of other centuries with styles, vocabulary, and the like that were so complicated that premodern English seemed like a foreign tongue. Likewise, I explored conversational, modern-lifestyle books, which were written like blog posts—very short, almost like a dialogue taken directly from the web to print.

Instead of my passport collecting more stamps, my personal library gained volumes. That year, I spent more money on purchasing books and shipping them back to my home in Florida than ordering additional pages for my passport. How I should have paid for those books with all the leftover Pesos, Pounds, and Euros cluttering our already hard-to-shut junk drawer in Florida.

ROLLING OUT THE UNWELCOME MAT

AFTER NEARLY TWO AND HALF MONTHS IN MASSACHU-
setts with quick visits to Poughkeepsie for doctor's appointments and for my birthday, my stay suddenly came to an
abrupt, uncomfortable halt.

I noticed that Frank and my mom had begun fighting
about random items, as minor as the dog, dinner, or the
mail. I could only imagine how much the stress of having
an unplanned guest—and an injured guest at that—was
enhancing all the tension.

One night after a typical dinner together in the living
room on TV trays with back-to-back *Seinfeld* episodes, I
left my mom and Frank for a "wine phone" date with my
friend Adriana. We stayed up talking about Thanksgiving,
her family, health issues—for once hers, not mine—and
plans for her birthday. We talked, laughed, and drank wine
until nearly midnight needing to plug in our phones for
more juice. It was the first time I felt like a normal friend

listening to her talk about her life and not just explaining my woes, pains, and situation. By the end of our wine phone date, both my mom and Frank had gone to bed. Having finished a bottle of wine while having a great time escaping my situation, I was a little more than tipsy. However, I wasn't driving. I only needed to go to bed and perhaps sleep well for once.

The next day, Mom informed me, "Frank says the wine is off limits. He thinks you've had too much to drink lately."

Shocked that my mom was the one telling me this instead of Frank, and surprised I would be judged about something as trivial as drinking, I responded, "Okay, that's fine. You can tell him he surely knows how to make me feel welcome. Maybe I have outstayed my time here."

I wasn't just extremely upset; I was frickin' pissed, fuming mad. If I could have hit or kicked something with all my former might, I would have, but I'd only hurt myself in the process. No one could comprehend what I was going through while under this forced house arrest. *I wanted a shred of independence back.* Even an adolescent had more freedom than I did as a severely physically and emotionally injured adult staying in someone else's home.

Although I didn't say I was leaving, my mom knew I wouldn't feel comfortable in a house where I couldn't be treated like an adult with respect and honest, open communication. My comment about not feeling welcome combined with the look on my face threw my mom into a tizzy. She started to yell at Frank that I was leaving because of him.

Without anywhere else to go in the moment, I went to my room. I was dumbfounded that in my condition, at the age of thirty-three, I had to stay in someone else's home and not on my terms. This was no way for me to recover. I had a broken neck, not broken pride. I needed to get out of the house.

Later that evening, when Frank came to my room, I said, "Well, it's obvious I've outstayed my welcome. This is your house. I'll remember that."

"You are always welcome, anytime. I love you."

After he left my room, my mom entered, sat down on my bed, and cried.

"I'm leaving!" I hadn't yet told AJ what had happened, but I knew he would not be happy. Any macho Latino takes offense when someone else mistreats his family, regardless of how he treats his own family. AJ and I spoke that evening. And I was right. He was raging mad about it. But he didn't waste any time picking me up the very next morning.

I was rescued from one house arrest and moved to another in New York. There, I would be faced with relying on the man who had hurt me more than the evil tree. House arrest in New York had its own set of challenges that I didn't admit to anyone.

For my mom and me, the separation was very difficult. Not only was it unexpected and quick, but we had also been looking forward to spending the holidays together. She had decorated the house beautifully and baked all of my favorite cookies from Russian teacakes to spritz. It felt like I was going to relive holidays from my childhood at home in Wisconsin.

However, because of the circumstances, I spent the rest of my recovery that winter in our studio apartment in the slums of Hudson River's not-so-finest city, Poughkeepsie.

There, I did my best to continue my recovery in a different setting keeping my spirits up by walking, reading, and talking to my clan. I finished each day by enjoying a couple of glasses of wine. AJ clearly said that, in our house, I could do what I wanted. So, cheers to wine in my house, regardless of still being on house arrest in New York and not in my real home in South Florida.

Was my glass half full or half empty? In either case, there was always room for more wine.

MALL THERAPY

AS MY ONLY PHYSICAL THERAPY WAS TO WALK DAILY, I DID it religiously. In general, I missed only on days I knew I would be wiped out from either a long car ride or a day full of doctor appointments with a mixture of good and bad news and more waiting. I had taken most of my walks on the Walkway Over the Hudson in Poughkeepsie, the Chelmsford bike trail in Massachusetts, and on my mom's treadmill. However, when I moved back to the studio apartment, I didn't have the luxury of a treadmill if the weather was bad. Thus, I did what I associate with elderly exercise.

Have you ever gone to a mall before it opens and seen elderly couples walking the concourses? Well, I have. And I've always applauded them for doing so. That winter, I joined their ranks; I started mallercise.

A handful of times, I needed to be driven to the Poughkeepsie Galleria to walk. I called a cab and rehashed my story with the driver, as it was hard to completely disguise the brace even with winter attire. The first lap or two of the mall was fine as I took in the layout, the changed storefront windows, sales, and the small coffee shops and food court. But walking the mall paled in comparison to the outdoors or even a TV in front of a treadmill. There were only so many times I could count garbage cans, fire extinguishers, or security cameras.

During our communal mallercise time, I imagine the elderly walkers wondered why someone my age was among them. However, it didn't take them very long to notice my large accessory, the cage, which explained my ailment. They, like many others, assumed I had been in a car accident. How I wished it had been so easy to explain, but no way Jose. There was no thirty-second version of my falling tree limb story.

The mallercise walks became another form of therapy necessary for my recovery as well as an escape from my house arrest. I had to be physically busy enough to let my mind wander from the discomfort, deception, and the waiting game until my next doctor's appointment.

JUST LIKE JASON BOURNE

Like Jason Bourne, the famous American spy played by Matt Damon in movies such as *The Bourne Identity*, I could go anywhere and know where the bathrooms and the nearest exit were, which person was staring at my cage, and, of course, where the lowest tree limbs were. Granted, I wasn't trained to kill or survive with expert driving, shooting, and fighting skills. But like Bourne's, my perception of the world had been fine-tuned because of my situation.

Although I had always been instinctually vigilant, during my recovery, I turned into a mini-Bourne, focusing on my surroundings more than ever, even though my cage limited my line of sight. I could see in front of me, but not much above my height, five foot five on a good day, or below my waist.

In addition, I could see for perhaps ten to fifteen feet to my right or left because everything else required me to move my body. My observation process was like that of a rotating lawn sprinkler, frequently changing angle of sight and then returning to the starting position to get the full picture. Although the lawn sprinkler dance is funny on the dance floor, my observation process was not.

Because of my inhibited sight as well as different surroundings, I found myself constantly surveying—taking in the people who were also at the doctor's office and pharmacy, wondering who they were, why they were there, and where the nearest chair was to rest my less-than-energetic body. On my daily walks outside, I didn't pass a tree that I didn't glance at to see if any partially fallen limbs could clobber me again. I found the wind scary as well, not knowing what it could possibly throw my way.

However, in the neighborhoods I walked daily, I had more to worry about than trees and wind. In Chelmsford, there was always a neighbor's dog running out and barking at me or a country-road driver zipping along way above the thirty-five-mile-per-hour limit and too close to the shoulder of the road. In Poughkeepsie, it was the inhabitants of the downtown area: the local crazies, the homeless, the shady drug dealers, or someone just released from the police station for who-knows-what offense. It wasn't hard for me to take it all in and then avoid it.

I didn't find an assassin, secret exit, or a pot of gold at the end of a rainbow through my observations. After all, I was new to the Bourne identity and espionage life. However, the observation skills honed that winter continued throughout my recovery.

STICKS AND STONES
WILL BREAK MY BONES
BUT WAITS WILL NEVER
HURT ME

IT WAS TRUE. A VERY LARGE STICK DID BREAK MY BONES. However, the delays and waiting I experienced would not hurt me—or at least not for long.

Indeed, waiting was disappointing and even depressing, but I chose to reframe the situation and thus my experience. It didn't mean I didn't feel low on some days. Every last ounce of patience was tested by Dr. Z, the disability caseworker, or even the brace man notifying me of another hurdle. Sometimes I cried, but more often, I dropped a few f-bombs and then stormed off for a walk to clear my head. I adapted my expectations of the near future by inserting the new hurdle and adjusting to the inevitable wait in my mental calendar.

Clearly, the wait was the only way to get back to my freedom and my life as I previously knew it. However, it didn't mean getting there by wallowing in self-pity. With much support through the process, reframing different circumstances, and digesting fresh unwanted information, I made it through the change of seasons and the celebrations of birthdays and holidays as I walked into a New Year.

If a clarity or truth came from this process, it was this: You cannot speed up nature. When you try, you will fail. Nature has a proven method of doing the most miraculous things such as repairing bones, wiping away bruises, and teaching muscles to function again. And it all takes time.

In my case, with the green leaves turning brilliant autumn colors and then falling and being covered with snow and ice, I witnessed seasons changing. Perhaps my body and its repairs were following the rhythm of the seasons. Would it be spring when my body felt free to dance and run again?

I found comfort in the wise words of Ralph Waldo Emerson: "Adopt the pace of nature. Her secret is patience."

Resign from Your Position

AT THE BEGINNING OF THE THIRD MONTH OF MY LEAVE OF absence from work, I needed to speak to the human resources department about various issues that only the director could resolve. Via phone, Beth, the newly appointed HR director and still rather inexperienced, explained we were coming up to an important date—ninety days of leave of absence. I didn't know it at the time, but ninety days is the longest period someone can be out on a leave of absence status. And my ninetieth day was, in fact, the last day of the year.

She said, "Heidi, I will need your letter of resignation."

When I heard the request, I was taken aback. I identified with this job. I was an impeccable employee who was well-liked both internally and externally by our partners. I was being hurt professionally by an accident that was in no way my fault. I took the request to resign as an insult. Although I knew Beth asked because she needed to for long-term disability coverage, it just wasn't done right. She seemed more concerned about following orders and getting my file done than my feelings. I hated that.

I didn't mention my dislike of that request, but I continued on with my other questions for Beth. However, afterward, I did talk to my circle of friends as well as legal counsel. It didn't feel remotely right or sensible to write my own resignation letter; my gut told me not to do it. And lo and behold, all of the lawyers told me not to resign, not to sign anything, and to provide only as much medical information as was relevant to the duration of the injury for my file.

In a second call to Beth, I told her, "I have put together all of the information you requested. However, I will not write a resignation letter."

Surprised, she paused and replied, "After the end of the year, I will assume your resignation because you didn't come back from your leave of absence." So, instead of me writing my own resignation letter, the company would go ahead, make an assumption, and progress the way it wanted to handle my case.

At the end of a traumatic year, yet again I had lost something important to me: my professional identity.

HAPPY NEW YEAR!

AFTER HAVING ONE HELL OF A YEAR, I FINALLY HAD reached the bottom of my emotional barrel.

Not only did that evil tree limb break my neck, but it also paused my life as I knew it. Because of the injury from the accident, I was unable to work for many months. I lost my job, a career path for which I had worked hard, and a marriage that could be saved only if I could look beyond the lies and hurt. When all the balls dropped, I found myself in a barrel, not exactly going over Niagara Falls, but in dire straits.

I had to find a way out of the dark, filthy barrel I was in—whether I had to climb, paddle, or just keep walking through the mucky mess to a new happy place. That evening—New Year's Eve—I resolved to recover physically, financially, and emotionally. It was the Matterhorn of multiple difficult resolutions, much harder than the typical vow to lose five pounds while faking the lyrics to "Auld Lang Syne" with a glass of bubbly in hand.

Speaking of bubbly, that particular New Year's Eve I celebrated in the studio with a bottle of cava, a sparkling wine from Spain. Likewise, in keeping with Spanish traditions, I ate twelve grapes at the stroke of midnight for good luck in the coming year. Although I was alone in the apartment as AJ was still at work, I received many messages, texts, and phone calls from my clan wishing me happiness in the coming year. I, too, wished for happiness.

In celebrating the New Year, I realized that without my clan, I wouldn't have triumphed. I told them I would take a rain check on a toast together, but until then, here's to a Happy New Year and climbing out of the bottom of the damn barrel.

archaic. Perhaps a good addition to the checkout process at the hospital would be sending patients home with a fax machine for all the documents to follow.

For the most part, I was of sound mind, so I completed the forms, sent them, and fielded the follow-up phone calls. However, I did not qualify for disability right away. There's always a paper pusher trained to find fault in a certain percentage of applicants—and that percentage included me and probably everyone else in need.

I believe there is something wrong with the whole process and the health care system itself. Despite my frustration, I didn't buy a fax machine. And I refuse to until it's covered by health care insurance.

WHEN WILL THEY MOVE
THE EVIL TREE?

AFTER NEARLY FOUR MONTHS, THE IMMENSE FALLEN LIMB
still took up space in the back of the Poughkeepsie apartment building. You would have thought the evil tree's owner
would have wanted to get rid of the limb as a hazard. It
served as a reminder of a major injury caused by the owner's
property. And most important to me, it added a pretty fat
in-your-face insult to my injury.

Regardless of why it was still there, that tree also
reminded me how lucky I was and that I survived to
breathe another breath. I was in awe each time I saw the
size of the limb, not to mention the height of the tree from
which it fell. I calculated it had plummeted from forty
feet, as the scar on the tree was even with the third and
fourth floors of the brick apartment building. Its length
was nearly twenty feet and it weighed almost a thousand
pounds. That weight, combined with the force of the drop,
made me cringe.

Instead of my dead body being yet another chalk outline, I was alive. A miracle.

Before my third appointment with the doctor, my mom came up to Poughkeepsie. I told her, "Mom, I'd like a piece of the tree to remember."

"I want to save a part of it in remembrance, too. How should we to do it?"

A chainsaw was expensive to buy for just one use. Plus, we didn't know anyone in the neighborhood well enough to borrow a saw. On the phone with my father that same day, when I mentioned cutting a piece of the tree, he said, "Why don't you buy a cheap handsaw?"

So off my mom and I went to Home Depot to buy a twenty-dollar handsaw. On that bone-chillingly cold January day, armed with a new handsaw, she cut a piece about a foot-and-a-half long and six inches around. It took nearly half an hour, but the result was a beautiful hefty piece weighing more than fifteen pounds. Afterward, she collected about a dozen branches—long, skinny ones; short and stubby ones; crooked ones—which she'd arrange in a large vase as a sculptured piece honoring my survival and life.

We anticipated someone from the building or the neighborhood would ask about the quasi-lumberjack event in the middle of downtown Poughkeepsie, but they didn't. That's for the best. Both of us felt anxious about the next day's doctor's appointment. And we felt a certain raw bitterness seeing the evil tree limb. Plus, we were armed with a handsaw. It likely wouldn't have been a positive confrontation.

As my mom packed up the saw, I looked at the tree

and wondered when I'd return to Poughkeepsie. AJ would come back for his schooling at the CIA. Although it would be unlikely he'd live in the same building, I knew revisiting the accident site would be in order, if only to wager a large sum to say no one would move that limb.

Because that tree had tried to take my life, to remember it, I had to take a piece of it too.

HOURS WITHOUT MY CAGE

AFTER ONE HUNDRED AND FOURTEEN DAYS—NEARLY FOUR months—I was cleared by Dr. Z at my third appointment to return home, start taking off the brace little by little, and shower again.

Eager to test life without the brace, I immediately took it off upon entering the studio, removing Velcro after Velcro strap until the shell was unleashed. It was like the freedom I felt when I got my braces off at sixteen but a full-body experience and intensified.

I felt much lighter and just free. But although I was happily released from my cage, I was also scared; my security blanket was temporarily gone. Regardless, it was a moment of pure happiness. Finally, I could take an unlimited, full exhale and inhale.

I found that lying down once again was relaxing, not uncomfortable as it had been for months. And I could scratch my back where a few days previously, I'd scratch it by rubbing against a corner like a bear in the forest would rub against a tree trunk.

Although I had the brace off for only a couple of hours the first day, it felt like I had been released from captivity. Granted, I knew I'd have to ease myself into a couple of hours off and a couple of hours on to help the rehabilitation of my back, shoulders, and neck muscles. But who cares! Little by little, I was getting my freedom back.

In just those few hours, I almost needed to get reintroduced to my own body. I imagine it's somewhat like carrying a child for nine months and then finally getting your body back to normal. However, I only had to take care of myself and not an infant. If AJ had had his wishes, I would have been knocked up, too. Thank my lucky stars I waited and thus dodged a major bullet.

At first, I was reluctant to nod my head because of its months of immobility. It was what I was supposed to be doing, but it took time to feel comfortable stretching the limits of my body after time served in my cage. I hoped that shortly this reluctance, too, would subside as other anxieties had in this process.

To celebrate, we all went out to dinner—my mom, AJ, and I—at the CIA's finest, reservations-only, haute Italian cuisine restaurant, Caterina de Medici. It was my first time in public without a brace. After four months with a partial view, I could see the world again in full-screen mode without rotating my torso or pointing my chair in a particular direction. I no longer needed a sippy cup for wine since my arm, neck, and torso could all work together to sample this liquid enjoyment. And just like the rite of passage at a Thanksgiving family meal, I had finally graduated to the adult table. I ate freely without spilling on my collar.

With my neck amazingly free to breathe, my scar, which was three inches long on the front of my neck, was visible. That night wasn't only my coming out party, but also my scar's first spin around the block. Only earlier in the day did I get my first glimpse of it. I thought it would be straight, but it was a tad curved. It had been covered up with a bandage to keep clean and a scarf for warmth over the past months. And it would remain with me for life.

That night, I wanted to show it off. Cheers to my badge of honor!

My Homecoming

ONLY DAYS AFTER MY SUCCESSFUL DOCTOR'S APPOINT-
ment, my mom and I arrived at Boston's Logan Airport to
travel to South Florida for my homecoming.

Four months earlier, I had arrived in Poughkeepsie only
with a red roller board carry-on. I returned home with
more baggage, both figuratively and literally, checking two
uber-large suitcases filled with health care paperwork,
greeting cards, gifts, and winter sweaters, hats, scarves, and
boots.

Most important, I was still donning my cage. I thought
I could ease my way out of the brace more quickly than
I did. Life without it was not as freeing as I first thought.
It was a tremendous amount of work to support my own
body. Plus, I was apprehensive about moving, timidly and
cautiously changing my position ever so slowly. I had been
forced into compliance for months, so it would take con-
scious effort and more pain to truly shed the brace. And by
no means would I fly in an airplane without it for support.

Out of habit, I was more comfortable with my cage than without.

Eager to return home, I had been counting down the days since the previous month while anticipating that my health would be improved enough to allow travel. I boarded the plane happy to be leaving my house arrest in New York and Massachusetts and eager to return to Fort Lauderdale. On seeing my cage, many from TSA security, the airline, and even passengers asked if I was okay. At that point, I was used to the looks of pity and concern. When I told them, "I'm finally returning home after four months," their faces changed to relief and delight for me. I vividly remember a passenger across from me, a thin, middle-aged man with gray hair who assisted with my overhead baggage. I had never before understood how helpful such a kind gesture could be.

The passenger's help caused me to flash back to when I was a high school teacher and led the school's Diversity Club. One year, we designed a Diversity Day. Club members assumed disabilities like blindness (blindfolded), hearing-impairment (protective ear covers), physical handicap (in wheelchair), left-handedness (not using dominant hand), and other handicaps for an entire school day. Afterward, we held a school assembly in a talk-show-style format. As the host, I invited the club members to share their experiences, challenges, and recommended changes to accommodate all abilities. Being the staff leader, I didn't take the challenge myself at that time. Instead, I had my own Diversity Day challenge with my real-life, multimonth recovery.

When I arrived in Fort Lauderdale, I smiled, recognizing the beach, the canals, and even the Everglades. Although I'd never been fond of the topography of Florida, I welcomed the sight of the place I'd been unable to return to for so long. With the help of the gentleman beside me once again, my mom and I deplaned and gathered my physical baggage. I carried my emotional baggage fairly well underneath my cage.

My dad awaited us to take me home. He hugged me with much less hesitation than before. "Welcome home, my favorite daughter." We loaded up the car for the last leg of my homecoming. Once again, my parents took one for the team by being cordial enough to ride in the same car. I imagine that each time they see each other, it's still emotionally unsettling. But thankfully during my recovery, they got past their own feelings to help me.

My homecoming ride through our neighborhood and seeing our home for the first time in months was exciting. I had lived in Florida for nearly five years, but after so much time outside of the area, it was weird seeing pink-, peach-, and Caribbean-colored homes. However, the palm trees and the hibiscus flowers were surely welcome sights after a dreary winter up north.

My father parked the car in the driveway and got my bags. I entered the front door of our two-story, peach-colored stucco house—just as I left it. But although it was our house, it didn't quite feel like it. I looked around at the pictures and artwork. Looking at our wedding photo above the entertainment center and a statue from our honeymoon in the living room corner, I sat down on the couch with bittersweet emotions. The warmth I remembered wasn't there. It had been frozen in time, but I had changed.

My parents noticed my reaction. They knew getting back into a normal routine—cooking, eating, showering, and sleeping—would bring a touch of that former "normal" back for me.

COMING CLEAN

AFTER MONTHS UP NORTH, WITH ALL OF MY FAMILY present, including AJ, I should have been happy at home. However, I was not.

AJ had driven down from New York to start his externship, which coincidentally was the same time I returned to Florida. It appeared to be a Hollywood happy ending with both of us simultaneously coming back to our home after such a terrible fall and winter. AJ posed to others that he chose his college externship to be in Florida so he could be with me, but I knew the truth. His selection came from his lack of other options.

With me out of work, he couldn't afford to live in Boston, New York City, or anywhere but in our Florida home while on an unpaid externship. He was not a hero; it was quite the opposite. Plus, I was sick and tired of patiently waiting for him to tell me the truth. While in New York and Massachusetts, I didn't have enough strength to deal with it; I had bigger fish to fry. However, the truth was always with me like a weeping wound, hidden beneath my cage.

Now that we were in our Florida home, I needed the truth.

Fortunately for me, my mother had traveled from Boston to Fort Lauderdale to help me ease into life with my limitations. She stayed an extra week with us without knowing what she was getting herself into. Within a day of AJ's returning, I started demanding what I rightfully should have gotten when I found the letter. Through witnessing firsthand our fights and AJ sleeping on the couch, she was worried. Finally, while we were on a walk, she asked me, "What is going on with you and AJ? Why all the fighting?"

I confessed. "Mom, he cheated on me."

She wanted to know more, but I didn't go into detail. When we returned home, I called my dad to come over to the house. I told both of my parents about AJ's infidelity and the letter I found the day before the evil tree fell on me. Enraged and deeply hurt, they couldn't believe I'd hidden such a huge piece of the puzzle for so long.

"I don't know what to do," I said. "Should I forgive him? He was there for me through my recovery, but he had lied for so long. Plus, he hasn't had the decency to come clean to me."

All I knew was I had to start emotionally dealing with it all, so my first step was to come clean to those who wouldn't make me feel ashamed.

At the time, my parents had been divorced nearly twenty-five years. Not unlike other divorced couples, they had grown apart during their eighteen-year marriage. In that time, infidelity was involved as well, so they had experience with my situation firsthand. I wouldn't think you would want your ex in the room when you were sharing your thoughts and feelings with someone who was going through marital strife. What an uncomfortable mess for them! No wonder my dad refilled his scotch various times.

Around the kitchen island, I shared the intimate details I knew about AJ's lies and betrayal. Of course, I also had to justify why I kept silent after my accident. They were upset I'd kept them in the dark until that evening. My mom cried; my dad was so pissed, he appeared ready to go on a manhunt. He had never liked AJ, but after my confession, he had reason to hate him and wish him harm.

Then they both hugged me. What could they say? AJ's lies had been revealed. Instead of being a valiant knight during my recovery, he was seen as yet another source of pain, stress, and hurt. But by unveiling the con man side of him, I had finally come clean about my harmful secret.

DAY OF SEPARATION

AFTER SEVERAL NIGHTS ON THE COUCH AND CONSTANT fighting, AJ approached me as he got ready for work.

"We should separate. I can crash at a friend's house."

I didn't want him to just up and leave, but I didn't want him to stay either. I was hurt but relieved that I could have time away from our fights and constant tension. That was until he told me the stipulation.

"This is a separation. No dating!"

The nerve—we were still married, and I was considering forgiving him. If that wasn't enough, in my condition, recovering from the accident, unable to drive, easing myself out of the brace, and unemployed, I was not about to date. I wasn't ready to make any decisions, let alone such a large one to divorce him and throw myself into the changed dating world.

Shocked by his request, I didn't ask any questions at the time. However, I wondered if his stipulation was to cover his fear of losing me, or to make sure I didn't act like he would during the separation and begin seeing a lover. I bet on the latter.

The following morning, he left with a car full of essentials to go stay with his friend from school. I went outside as he pulled out of the driveway in our silver Honda. That's when he rolled down the window and said, "I'm sorry. I'm really sorry." Then he lit a cigarette, put on his sunglasses, and drove away. Sobbing, I returned inside to the couch where my mom was waiting.

"Mom, was that good-bye? 'Cause it sure feels like a termination, not a temporary separation. He has finally stepped out the door with both feet." She continued to hug and rock me until I calmed down.

Did he know what my decision would be before I did?

Three-Legged Bar Stool

I FELT WOBBLY, OFF-BALANCE, AND UNSTABLE AS IF I WERE an uneven three-legged bar stool with no leg completely touching the ground. My career leg was cut off, my health leg was at three quarters, and my relationship leg was cut in half. My friends and family were strong, but AJ and I were separated.

Not unlike Mount Washington's weather and winds, my bar stool would tilt unpredictably, leaving me guessing which direction and when. Shockingly, when there was growth in one of the areas of my recovery, another area would regress. It was like one step forward and two steps back.

I never expected my physical therapy without the brace to be so painful. And it was the same one step up and two or three steps back with my emotions. I never could have dreamt of the emotional roller coaster I rode on—like having an all-year, all-access pass to an amusement park ride called "It's a Small, Screwed-Up World After All." I just wanted to get off.

And I wanted my three-legged bar stool to be on even ground.

Perhaps that goal wasn't realistic. Can you ever have all three legs even on the ground? Maybe it's normal to be unbalanced. Would we all make up for some of the imbalance with crutches of some sort? At the time, I would have been okay jerry-rigging my bar stool with wads of napkins or matchboxes as if fixing a wobbly table at a restaurant.

Could someone stop playing "It's a Small World After All"? I wanted to escape this tilt-a-whirl ride.

Everything Reminds Me of Him

It had been almost ten years since we met. We had been living together for eight years and of those years, we were married four. We went through moving into apartments in Boston and then to Florida, buying our first home, through various stages of education, new jobs, layoffs, surgeries, and vacations. Every movie, song, picture, piece of furniture, souvenir, even my cell phone number had a connection to him.

Because I was so distraught with the clusterfuck I was going through, all of those things were triggers that made me feel trapped. I wished I could just get away to a place removed from everything associated with us or him.

Ten years was a full third of my life. Granted, I had changed much and grown in that time, but I thought I was always changing *with* him and vice versa. Now, my memories just seemed like a waste.

I tried to limit the reminders that blatantly made things

worse, such as our wedding photos and his clothes. I took off my wedding rings and placed my grandmother's wedding ring on my left hand to give me strength. A college graduate when women didn't go to the university, this woman was stoic and took no bullshit.

I just couldn't stop the recurring racing thoughts of various interactions between the other woman and him. Had she been in our house and in our bed? It was like a skipping record in my mind interrupted by waves of sanity from a phone call with my clan or a book that took me away from my wicked reality.

Although many people told me this wasn't true, I thought of a scene in the musical *Avenue* Q, which AJ and I had seen together in New York City the summer before. I remembered this line: "Was it love or just a waste of time?" I knew *intellectually* that all of our time together wasn't a waste, but it sure felt like it. Now at thirty-three, I needed to pick up the pieces of my life. Still, I was dependent on my parents like a teenager.

Where am I? Can I be a better person because of this? Will I ever trust anyone again? How can I navigate through this? Please resurface strong enough to get through this. I can't spend my life feeling miserable.

My life was in shambles.

Unloading Baggage to Someone Impartial

Since my parents didn't have enough time to listen to my story day in and day out, and I didn't feel comfortable telling my friends yet, I needed to talk to someone who would be impartial.

I also needed another reason to get out of the house. So after various uncomfortable phone calls to local mental health centers, I found a counselor, Virginia. She was an attractive Latina in her early forties, remarried, and a mother. And best of all, her office was within walking distance of our house.

Upon entering Virginia's office, I was still in my cage, sleep deprived, and a bundle of unpredictable nerves. Although a portion of what we talked about the first time was the physical accident, it didn't take too long to get to the real story and my turmoil: my failed marriage.

Not a stranger to an adulterer's tricks and lies, Virginia

told it to me straight—not as a family member, not as a friend, but as a professional woman.

She, too, had gone through something similar with a cheating spouse. She restated things I already knew, but I needed to hear them again and again to internalize them. I knew my emotions had gotten the best of my sanity and me.

"Heidi, you need to be valued by someone who will stand by you because he *wants* to, not because he *needs* to for schooling, money, citizenship, or other things. Do you think AJ could have gone to CIA without your financial help and your family's loans?"

Ashamed, I looked at her and said, "He said he loved me. I think he did, but he used me. And he still is. How can a husband or even a friend who loves me do this?"

"You can be valued by AJ or by someone else."

Each hour with Virginia seemed to race by with more to tell in the sessions that followed. Oh how I dreaded the clock's timer indicating our session was up. My half-hour walks home became my processing time. That's when I replayed details of what I had shared and what she had said in response.

Ironically, I had sought out counseling once before; it was with AJ early in our relationship. I should have noticed the red flags long, long before we married or even moved to Florida. However, as a type A woman, I tried so hard to make it work that I overcompensated for all his insufficiencies. I even started to change myself into a person who would be not so headstrong, not so independent, and not so social.

What was I thinking? I needed a smacking.

TRYING EVERY TECHNIQUE

BEFORE MY FULL-BLOWN LIFE CATASTROPHE, I NEVER understood being unable to let my mind rest or sleep.

It was clear I'd been lucky; I had never been truly obsessed or troubled before. I could typically get over disappointment, embarrassment, and fights with time, but I never lost sleep over it. I never needed to try multiple techniques and medication to stop the obsessive-compulsive daydream and nightmare sequences.

However, during my melodramatic saga of recovery, I tried damn near everything. I turned to CDs for meditation at home and on my iPhone away from the distractions in a nearby park. I read every book about recovering from traumatic injuries to divorce and loss. The bookshelves in my office and living room looked like a full-fledged self-help bookstore.

I also purchased a zafu, a special meditation pillow, which ironically resembled a hemorrhoid cushion. I went to restorative yoga class for injured people multiple times a week. I took prescribed Valium for months. I did acupuncture, massage, and the good old bartender's cure, booze. Plus, I wrote in a journal, which was a collection of completely illegible entries from angry lists of lies to whining and run-downs of daily events. To my credit, after years of texting and typing, whose handwriting is any better than chicken scratches anyway?

What helped numb the brain best was my nightly sleeping pill. At first, I was scared to take them, but I remembered my former boss used to take the same pills for transatlantic flights. Plus, my father said he used sleeping pills much stronger than my prescription while recovering from his divorce.

Ahhhhh…the little magical pills allowed me to sleep eight heavenly hours each night. I had somehow survived the previous months of discomfort and just plain disjointed sleep caused by my cage and pain. However, in coming to terms with a failed marriage, I couldn't sleep as my mind obsessed about his lies, replayed our memories, and hung on to my embarrassment and shame. The pills provided a much-needed reprieve from the constant conversation, flashbacks, and what-if scenarios going on the rest of the day.

I hoped I would not need these pills for long, but I knew the fastest way for me to go insane would be through sleep deprivation. I needed to have as clear a head as I could. Sleep was just one of the ingredients needed to make me get the strength to know what I'd do with my three-legged bar stool.

FALLING INTO
OLD PATTERNS

IT HAD BEEN A WEEK SINCE AJ LEFT, YET I HAD BEEN waiting for his call for days.

I stayed up late replaying the past and questioning it all. Was he going to try to win me back? How long would he wait? How could I be falling into my old patterns of waiting for crumbs of affection? Finally, I gave up and took a sleeping pill.

The next day, while trying to take a midafternoon nap, I envisioned myself on a beach, gentle waves kissing the sand, and all alone in a hammock. Still, he kept popping into my dream. And then BAM, he actually called.

Nervous, I answered.

"Heidi, I want to work on this. With time apart, I know what I want. I love you."

Rather surprised he didn't want to throw our relationship away, I tried to remain calm and replied, "I need more time."

First, I needed to build myself back. So fueled by Virginia's advice, I said, "I need to be valued by someone who is there not because he *has* to be or it's easy, but because he *wants* to be. I have given you so much; I have nothing left to give."

For the first time, he said, "Let me give back to you. I don't want a divorce."

Then he asked, "Am I still a part of your life?"

I wanted to scream at his stupidity. What an arrogant thing to ask! I was the one still in our house. And I was the one who had been faithful. He simply said, "I'm sorry. I made mistakes." However, he didn't say anything about all of the things he had been hiding or lying about. I wanted to angrily grill him, but I didn't. I just cried.

Then in my shaky voice, I managed to say, "I'm glad I have family and friends to support me."

"I support you."

I laughed. With fierce spunk, I said, "You did not support me for the past year with your other woman and focusing on school. Now, when I need you most, you aren't here either!"

Afterward, I told him he could come to the house only with my permission. He repeated what I said rather sarcastically because he was upset, but he had no other option but to agree.

Could I trust him? I certainly didn't know who he was anymore. In fact, to keep AJ out, I had my locks changed as well as the frequency in the garage door opener. Plus, I didn't know how bat-shit crazy the other woman was. There have always been a bunch of crazies in Miami, heck the entire state of Florida. I wouldn't put it past her to do something psycho.

That day, although I was glad I picked up the phone, it was clear I was too emotionally involved to make any decisions or to have a real talk. I first had to find who I was and what I wanted. I didn't need to fall down the slippery slope that got me into this mess before I could talk to him again.

He knew exactly how to push me one way or the other. A good con man.

A Text for Valentine's Day

To date, my worst Valentine's Day ever happened that year.

I was bombarded with loads of Valentine's wishes via Facebook, marketing e-mails, mass texts, and even random couples sending save-the-date cards. Nauseous from my gut-wrenching anger, I felt like puking, but instead I threw my coffee cup across the room. From my Macbook, I ranted, "Those of us who don't have anyone or worse, a cheating SOB husband, certainly don't want to be reminded all day that we have nobody special. Please tell your partners, not the world."

Then I got up, walked across the room, and threw all of the cards in the trash.

After getting off my soapbox and cleaning up the broken coffee mug, I received a text from AJ that threw me into a deeper level of distress. It simply read, "Happy V-Day!"

So, I paused. Really? This was what I deserved after ten years? A text for Valentine's Day? I didn't know what to do. Should I respond, should I ignore it, or what? I certainly didn't want to respond in a happy fashion—"Happy Valentine's Day, my dear husband and love of my life!"—because it wasn't a joyous Valentine's Day. It wasn't even remotely close to my thoughts at the time. And he was not a dear husband. Neither did I want to be truthful about how sad, depressed, and outright angry I felt or I'd text, "Thanks for making this the worst Valentine's Day ever!"

What I needed was a text-activated taser; just a slap in the face wouldn't do. So with the only iota of civility I had left, I sent back, "Thanks. Got your text."

I couldn't believe it. Was I asking too much for Valentine's Day from my husband? Oh hell no! *I wanted him to fight for me.* Despite our agreement to give me time, I wanted action that showed I meant more to him than a text. *Pick up the damn phone and call me, buy me chocolates, send me flowers, or all of the above.*

I wished the day had already ended. Happy F****** Valentine's Day!

PANIC ATTACK

NOTHING HELPED ME REALIZE HOW MENTALLY AND EMO-tionally fragile I was than when I experienced a panic attack that Valentine's Day while riding with my dad on I-95.

We set out to attend the Miami International Boat Show, a yearly tradition to view the boats we wished we owned but couldn't afford. I thought I could help him as a copilot while driving to Miami in the fast, high-volume traffic. However, wearing my brace, I felt like a horse with blinders going seventy-five-plus miles per hour in four lanes of traffic.

So rather precariously, the two of us, one with blinders and the other not such a confident South Florida driver, headed to Miami for a nerve-racking ride. I held on for dear life without the ability to do anything except panic.

Seeing my reaction as we exited I-95 and came to a stoplight, Dad said, "Maybe we shouldn't have come." I felt bad, but I was scared in my cage and in a small little clown car next to dozens of Mack trucks. However, since it was my first time to Miami in months as well as the afternoon of a wretched Valentine's Day, I had to continue. I needed to be busy. I especially couldn't think about AJ's text from that morning.

Although a little emotionally bruised and battered, we arrived at the marina with its hundreds of booths, dozens of food stands, and masses of tanned Australian, Kiwi, and South African yachties, eager yacht salesmen, and of course potential buyers or wannabes with eye-candy dates on their arms, all amongst millions of dollars' worth of toys. We walked down the first dock and took off our shoes to view a catamaran. To board, we'd have to step off the dock about three feet onto the boat.

Nervously, I looked at the dock and then at the boat. And just like that, I chickened out. My dad as well as the staff of the catamaran tried to help. I declined assistance and let my dad take the tour solo. I realized then, on that dock in Miami, I was weak and still broken. I used to be the first to get on a boat, scuba dive, flip people off jet skis, and the like. Only a half-year ago, that came as second nature.

Will I overcome these fears? Will I always live like this? Can I regain the ballsy persona I once had?

I'm not well enough to even call myself *me*.

The only good thing about the day was a little distraction and a call from Adriana, who was raising a newborn, interviewing for a faculty position, and finishing her PhD. It didn't necessarily make my situation look good, but it grounded me to the fact that others had trying and stressful lives. However, to her credit, she had a loving husband who shared the burden of all of the good and all of the bad. She was juggling another version of having it all—family, health, career—albeit with challenges but also with an all-in partner.

After eavesdropping on our conversation, my dad chimed in, "Heidi, just like Adriana, when you can share the work or weight, you can do four times the amount."

I looked at him and said, "No shit! I've been a one-woman sherpa!"

Before leaving the show, I passed one of the trade show booths selling earphone and microphone sets for sailing couples. Designed so the couple didn't have to yell back and forth to one another from the bow to the stern, they were comically called "marriage savers." I broke up laughing.

What would be my marriage saver?

THE STRAW THAT BROKE THE CAMEL'S BACK

ONE DAY, NOT LONG AFTER STARTING COUNSELING WITH Virginia, she recommended I stop talking to AJ until I wasn't so emotionally fragile and knew clearly what to say.

"What he started by leaving the house was good. It wasn't for a divorce or for dating, but to give you space to figure yourself out." I was worried I needed to make a decision soon or at least before he returned to school after his externship, which would be in three months.

Knowing I felt time-pressured, Virginia reminded me, "You don't have to be on anyone's time line. You take whatever time you need to get perspective." Also, she hinted I should stop worrying about life's little technical things such as paperwork and anything that didn't have to do with my recovery.

"All the little things can wait. And that means trying to find more details about the infidelity through phone records and e-mails."

One phrase echoed on my walk back home. She reframed my story for me. "The infidelity was just the straw that broke the camel's back. Your neck was the climax to make sure you took the time to realize this and learn to change."

ACTIONS SPEAK LOUDER THAN WORDS

My preliminary investigation of the con man started before the accident and ended with the letter. Then I was forced to pause my search.

My multiple-month hiatus was just long enough that I began believing the lies again. It was like Florence Nightingale syndrome, the caregiver falling in love with the patient, but in reverse—the patient loving a cheating caregiver again.

I lied to myself through the fall and winter, not sharing my story with family or friends, believing he really loved me. I didn't think it was that easy for him to say "I love you." I didn't think all of the conversations about his reasons for going away to college, his work schedule, his unknown phone calls, and his care for me during my recovery in New York were all lies. I didn't want to face what I knew deep down. I was in denial.

Returning to Florida caused me to change my channel. I started uncovering lies and more lies, seeing them for what they were and who he was. The hard facts, such as the notes left behind by the other woman found after he moved in with his friend and the phone calls or texts I caught through the monthly family-plan bill, weren't lies. I even flashed back to finding food items he hated in the studio apartment, specifically barbecue sauce.

Why didn't I realize then that someone else had been at the apartment? The physical evidence in the studio wasn't a lie either. Just like other adulterers, he was nailed because of his phone and her many notes, including that letter. But who would have thought to throw out the barbecue sauce as evidence? After all, it's a condiment. If it ain't empty, shove it back in the fridge.

The list of his lies was long, but so were his backup stories. At one point, I believed them because I loved him. And I was a good liar to myself, almost an accomplice. However, the proof was the condiment in the fridge next to the ketchup and mustard.

AJ, your actions speak louder than your words.

Telling My Friends

It felt like I was wearing the Scarlet Letter. I didn't commit adultery, but I felt ashamed.

I didn't want to share with my friends (or anyone else) that my husband had cheated on me. I was embarrassed. I didn't need to ask myself how it happened because I heard in my head my grandfather's Missouri accent saying over and over, "You sure look smarter than that." That's what he said when my father or uncle did something stupid.

I'm an intelligent woman. Maybe I should have known better. Maybe I looked smarter than I was. Regardless, I knew that because of his actions, I would be judged. What was wrong with me? How could I be so undesirable or not good enough to keep him?

In the twenty-first century, I couldn't come to terms with the unfairness of my shame. It was still a macho society. Instead of having him wear a tattoo or letter, he got to take off his wedding ring and walk free. So I had to be the one carrying my tail between my legs until I felt comfortable telling people.

Why do we feel ashamed when it's the cheating SOBs who should feel the shame? I hid it. Likewise, I learned that many women had hidden their stories from me. We would all be reluctant to share until we knew the other woman was part of the Scarlet Letter Club, too.

NAKED, HURT, AND ALONE

To AID MY SEARCH FOR CONTINUED HEALTH CARE IN Florida, I had to send an X-ray of my C-7 vertebra to Dr. Z in New York so he could approve the fusion of my bone and finally okay me for follow-up care.

After calling, verifying insurance, finding a location within walking distance, and making an appointment, I set out alone to an imaging center. That day I felt liberated, not needing to have my father or mother accompany me.

I entered the reception area and, like an old hat, filled out umpteen papers with all of my digits, names, addresses, ailments, and allergies. Then I waited with the other patients. We were all trying to size up each other. I was in my cage, so my hardship was clearly evident. I puzzled over some of them and then focused my attention on the live press conference on TV. Ironically, it was Tiger Woods's confession of his infidelity, complete with his apology.

I sat there as if I were his wife, a victim of a cheating husband, but at least I wasn't known on a global scale. In the waiting room, I held back tears. That's when I realized I'd made a mistake coming to the imaging center alone. Maybe I had stretched my newborn independence a little too far.

I listened to Tiger's words, but they were the same words AJ would utter in explaining his adultery. It didn't matter that all of the facts weren't the same; there were so many similarities. It was the only time in my life I would have preferred watching a dreaded infomercial with a B-list actor. The truth coming from a celebrity about his lies was hitting me deep under my cage and breaking my heart more than it already was.

My only savior was the imaging assistant who called me to enter the treatment room, allowing me to escape the press conference. There, the team of radiology techs treated me with caution knowing I had a neck injury. However, I told them, "I have a neck stronger than a football player's now. I'm not sure about the rest of me, but you don't have to be scared."

They asked me to take off my sweatshirt and brace so I could pose for multiple X-rays. These would be sent to my previous doctor as well as three possible follow-up-care doctors in Florida.

After positioning me, all three of the techs went back to their private room and closed the door. Then they turned on bright lights, making the rest of the room dark. I felt like I was under an intense investigation.

The room was cold. I was without my brace. I couldn't see them, but they could see me. Unable to move with the X-rays in process, streams of tears ran down my face falling onto my undershirt. It was a combination of the lights, the chill, and the news before entering the room that tumbled my emotions into freefall.

I felt so naked, hurt, and alone.

I continued to cry while I got dressed and exited the imaging room. I sat in the reception area to collect myself as the news commentators were replaying the key points of Tiger's apology. What torture! His words were bad enough, let alone the additional slides with bullet points highlighting his pleas for forgiveness. Come on. If Tiger Woods could come clean on international news, what about AJ?

I had to get out of there.

I quickly spoke with the receptionist, double-checking the fax numbers of all of the doctors and confirming the time and day the films would be ready. Then I began walking home—or at least to the place that used to feel like a home.

CARIS'S LOVING CONCERNS

CARIS, MY DEAR FRIEND FROM HIGH SCHOOL, WAS THE blue-eyed, blond next door who would knock people's socks off with her sharp intuition and wit.

Never wanting to be the last to know, she regretfully found out about my accident weeks after it happened from her sister, also a classmate and now a Facebook friend. Horrified and concerned she'd missed such terrible news, she immediately called. Drawing on her background in nursing as well as psychology, we talked primarily about how I felt, my pain, and my chances for complete recovery. After our brief early conversations, she hesitantly opened a Facebook account, not wanting to miss such important news ever again.

While continuing to call, Caris also started to send thoughtful care packages filled with books. Always a bookworm, Caris made choices that were not only entertaining but also motivational. It seemed as if the nickname she gave me when we were young—the wise one—should have been hers.

One time on the phone while I was still in Massachusetts, she said, "I think the accident was a way for you to wake up from your crazy schedule and life." Although it took time for me to realize it, she was entirely correct. I had bitten off more than I could chew. I had been attempting to conquer a perfect life: successful career, marriage, house, and two gym memberships to keep the extra pounds at bay. But maybe that's not the life that would make me happy. She knew that books filled with others' spins of unfortunate circumstances turned into humorous social perspective would be soothing as well as insightful. She kept USPS busy.

It wasn't until after Valentine's Day that I revealed to her (and a few other close friends) that the man I'd been relying on had betrayed me the most. With scars of her own from past relationships, Caris knew I didn't need this heartbreak on top of my pain and physical limitations. At the time, she was busier than I had ever been. With a two-year-old child, a seven-month-old baby, and a seven-year-old stepson, she was happily married, working full-time, and gearing up to go back to school. Thankfully, she still found time to call from her organized chaos in Wisconsin to my emotional basket case in Florida.

In our conversations, I shared details of my fights with AJ and my uncertainty about the future. Caris stressed that I didn't need to rush any decisions. "You don't have to push yourself to your perfect standards." It was true. I was partly to blame for all that was spiraling down. I chose the man. I chose the marriage. I chose the career. I chose it all.

At one point, she reminded me what a friend had said while I was studying abroad in Madrid. "Heidi, you could get along anywhere." Caris also reminded me that I was like a chameleon—adaptable and able to mold into this new situation, too.

Vulnerable and deeply wounded, I needed a reminder that I could adapt to *this* new life, too.

THE UNCOMFORTABLE OB-GYN'S COUCH

AFTER NEUROSURGERY, MULTIPLE CT SCANS UP THE YING, and the endless search for a continuing-care doctor down the yang in Florida, I needed to see yet another health care professional.

It was time for the joyful yearly exam with my OB-GYN; plus, I had some unprotected adultery to rectify. I admit the chance of STDs had concerned me before I returned to Florida, but I had a laundry list of other worries. What would it have mattered if I had herpes, syphilis, or worse? What if I had not survived the evil tree?

In Florida I started to smell the roses *and* the garbage. If I had an STD, what icing would it be on top of all the really bad cake I'd been served over the last months? So, I made the appointment that no woman ever anticipates with excitement unless she's trying to have a baby and was pregnant.

I had been a patient of my Eastern European OB-GYN

for nearly a decade. With a strong Slavic accent, she always asked about when I'd have kids. I kept responding that I wasn't ready. She looked at my chart and age with a disapproving look each time. However, this time, she asked, "What is the reason of your visit?"

"I'm here for my annual exam, a full STD check, and a prescription for a blood test. My husband has been cheating on me with another woman, unprotected for a year." You could tell by her face she recognized the story. I wondered how many times she'd heard it just that day.

"I'm so sorry. I will do everything and get the results to you as quickly as possible." Then she started the poking, prodding, and all of the uncomfortable parts of an OB-GYN visit, including butcher paper sheets, bristle brushes for tests, and putting your vagina in another person's face—not knowing if you had an STD or an impending fart.

After she finished the examination, she asked me again about the prescriptions she should write. I asked her only for the HIV blood test.

"Would you like another twelve months of your birth control?"

"No need. I have never felt so unsexy. And there's no chance I'll be having sex with my cheating husband again."

She reacted in the most unexpected way by saying, "I know you're hurt right now, but his actions do not have to mean the end of your marriage. Some people do get over this. They work through their differences. They learn to trust and love again."

Although some would have been happy to hear such encouraging words, I was in the mood for a powerful sound-off calling him out for his selfishness, lies, and actions. I wanted her to be as stoic and as matter-of-fact as she'd been over my many examinations. If anything, I thought she would have said something like, "Take him to the cleaners!"

However, once again, I was wrong. Who knows the reasoning behind her advice? Perhaps she was used to advising mothers-to-be who had more to lose than I did. Could it have been she had survived a cheating partner herself and had forgiven that person?

Of all of the couches I'd lain on confessing my failed marriage, hers was the most uncomfortable physically. And her emotional advice felt pretty useless. Sharing my strife typically made me feel better, but in this case, I left bitter and betrayed, not only by AJ but by my own kind.

GROUNDHOG DAY

NEARLY FIVE MONTHS AFTER LEAVING MY OFFICE TO HEAD up to Poughkeepsie, I returned to my old office in downtown Fort Lauderdale to collect my personal things. Still wearing my brace and not able to drive, I rode with my father who provided emotional support as well. It was strangely unfamiliar entering the same building and elevator as I had done thousands of times before.

With an announcement to the staff prior to my arrival, it turned out to be a warm welcome with many friendly faces, even from accounting and the depths of IT. However, all of the faces looked at me with tentative smiles. They don't teach people how to react to injuries and recovering patients in school. Nor are all people good actors. I could read their anxiety across their faces as well as through their questions: "Did you hear the tree falling? How long do you have to wear the brace? Have you started PT? When are you coming back?" Awkward questions for us all.

After socializing a bit, I was escorted back to my corner

office. Other than my house, it was the only part of my life that had remained untouched since I left. My outdated punch list still hung on the board. My desk was the cluttered chaos that I left, with manila folders and Post-its scattered in ways only I could find the needed info. It seemed like *Groundhog Day*—no, not the ridiculous holiday with Punxsutawney Phil predicting the length of winter but the Bill Murray movie that repeated the same day over and over.

I took a moment and sat in my rolling leather chair and looked out my office window at the New River, Las Olas Boulevard, parking garage, and helipad. How different would life have been if I hadn't gone to work remotely in New York that week?

Over the course of fifteen minutes, my dad and I collected my few books and two photos—one of AJ on our wedding day and the other a gift from a former coach stating, "I have no doubt." The visit gave me yet another glimpse into my previous reality.

As I left with one small box of items, I didn't feel quite ready to let my past career go. Could I possibly return and correct one of the legs of my three-legged bar stool when I was ready?

MAN KILLED BY TREE BRANCH IN CENTRAL PARK

NOT UNLIKE WHEN THE TREE FELL ON HALLOWEEN IN New Hampshire, my friends and family were reporting other accidents to me. I received a text from Diana regarding a horrible incident involving a tree branch in New York's Central Park. Evidently, the man killed was forty-six. Although the branch was much smaller than the limb that struck me, reports said the twenty-foot-long, hundred-pound branch fell from eighty feet.

I didn't remember the tree striking me. I didn't recall hearing a snap or anything that would tell me to get the heck out of Dodge. When I replayed that afternoon and taking out of the trash, I remember everything from leaving the apartment, passing the mailboxes, going down the stairs, feeling the cool moist air, and turning the corner to go through the parking area to the dumpsters. Then I went blank.

I wonder if the man in Central Park heard a warning.

Regardless, my doctor was right. I was lucky to have survived. It could have played out otherwise. I'd better take advantage of this second chance.

What needed to be different about my path to improve upon my previous mistakes so I could have it all—mostly happiness?

KNOWING ME BETTER THAN MYSELF

WHEN MY HUSBAND ARRIVED IN FLORIDA AFTER DRIVING down from New York for his externship, I immediately noticed a few things in his car that I'd specifically left packed for storage in Poughkeepsie for the following fall. Despite my asking him to place them in the storage facility, he didn't.

Why would he go to the trouble of unpacking my hair dryer, brush, and toiletries?

Then I realized he'd brought the items with a specific idea in mind. At that time, he knew me better than I knew myself. He knew I wouldn't be returning to New York to see him, nor would I be unpacking the storage facility with him. He didn't want to deal with sending my items back the following fall. He did it because he knew I was only steps away from a crucial decision about our relationship—to forgive or not forgive a cheater.

How did he know this before I did? Was I not truly

myself yet? I was living in a reality of recovery from issues larger than our marriage. I left the real me and put myself on pause to recovery physically. I even created a fantasy of forgiving my cheating husband for months, including hiding the truth from everyone. However, when more of my former reality—our house, friends, sights, and smells—started to slowly come back, I began evaluating the situation.

The answer for me would be to create another reality, distinct from my previous or even the forgiving fantasy-like reality of recovery up north.

Perhaps my next reality would be without him?

Left Hand Doesn't Know What the Right Hand Is Doing

To continue my health care—or rather self-care—I needed to transfer my medical records from New York. I started trying this when I first returned to Florida, thinking it would be rather easy.

In all honesty, I had done much harder things such as passing calculus and biochemistry in college, which were both Greek to me. Like a seasoned patient, I contacted the hospital directly to verify all of the correct numbers, departments, and names. Then I dutifully wrote and printed my consent letter and walked to the nearest fax. All my i's were dotted and t's crossed for them to send my medical records—or so I thought.

After completing my part, I received a phone call from the hospital. "Hi, this is Vanessa from St. Francis. We received your fax. We will get your medical reports to your new doctor, but your films cannot be sent this way. You will have to contact the radiology department directly." Knowing I couldn't fight the system, I hung up and called the radiology department, all the while thinking the situation was a complete fiasco.

The radiology department told me, "You must send a separate written release for us to send the films or copies." I paused and took a deep breath. Ahhhhhh…the oxymoron of "health care professional" was correct time and time again. With the two departments in the same building, they should have been on the same team. But it seemed as if each department was only accountable for its particular test, surgery, scan, or niche. Then each would pass the buck!

I used to proclaim that everyone should have to work in the service industry to learn how to deal with people. After my experience, I added that all should have to witness the terrible health care system to know how unhealthy, disjointed, and nonconducive to healing it is. Its left hand doesn't know what its right hand is doing, which hurts more than it helps.

All so-called health care professionals have a specific skill set or expertise—surgeon, lab tech, radiologist, dietician, physical therapist, anesthesiologist—but who is the foreman or the health care traffic controller? Could everyone cooperate instead of making me, the patient, work so hard? How could anyone heal in such a fragmented, cold environment?

I implore you: get on the same page without my needing to make numerous phone calls and send multiple faxes, letters, and e-mails!

CAPTAIN OF THIS SHIP

AFTER GETTING A CLEAN BILL OF HEALTH FROM DR. Z IN New York, successfully maneuvering through multiple hoops to get my health records to Florida, and then being rejected for follow-up care by several neurosurgeons and other specialists, I was desperate. I needed help.

I wanted to start the next step of recovery, which meant physical therapy. With throbbing knots in my neck and back, I was in pain physically, but was also emotionally distraught. Why did I have to work this hard to find a ready, willing, and able doctor? After weeks of countless searches for a continuing-care doctor, I was ready to give up and scream uncle. In fact, after an adult tirade at another potential doctor's office, the same doctor who rejected me gave me the name of another doctor not far from my home.

After explaining my case to the new doctor's secretary and of course waiting for his verdict, she called me back with an appointment for early the next week. After one full month of searching for continued care, I finally had an appointment!

My trusty chauffeur and dad drove me to the appointment, located in a not-so-good part of town in a converted strip mall. It featured random medical and legal offices as well as a cheap hot dog stand. After parking in the rear of the building, we stumbled upon the nondescript entrance. No sign or doctor's name, only a number. I entered the waiting room feeling skeptical.

In the small, twelve-seat room, a handful of patients sat quietly waiting. There was no TV, only reading material, plus a fake plant and a water cooler. The patients didn't look as serious as I did with my full set of armor, but they didn't look particularly healthy or wealthy either. Most appeared as if they were there for workman's comp.

Like a good patient, I walked to the closed receptionist's window and knocked. After I introduced myself, the receptionist asked me to once again fill out multiple pages of the same details I had filled out at every other health care facility from New York to Massachusetts to Florida.

Shortly after completing my forms, Dr. R, a short, trim man dressed in khakis and a doctor's coat, opened the door. "Will Heidi and her father come with me?" We followed him through the labyrinth of hallways lined with treatment rooms and storage closets, finally arriving at his small corner office. We got as comfortable as one can sitting in pain opposite a desk and waiting for a judgment. Dr. R refreshed his memory by paging through my bulky file. Meanwhile, I surveyed the walls and desk to get a read on Dr. R. I saw his medical school diploma, news clippings, photos of his family, and weird sci-fi memorabilia.

Although he'd reviewed my records before accepting the appointment, he took off his glasses and asked, "Heidi, why did you come to me today?"

I shared my story from the accident to recovering in Massachusetts and New York, not forgetting to include hurdles on my emotional roller-coaster ride such as not sleeping, relationship turmoil, and counseling sessions. He listened without interruption in spite of my wordy explanation. I had acquired so much medical and insurance lingo over my months, I couldn't tell the story in my own words without using phrases such as *pain level, high risk, preexisting condition,* and *bone fusion.*

While fighting back the tears, I said my final plea, "I'm here because no one will accept me as a patient. Please help me."

"I will help you."

As tears of relief ran down my face, he said, "I will help you recover. And, I mean the whole person, physically, emotionally, and mentally." He told me he understood what I was going through; he called it a life change. He shared with us that a year and a half earlier, he'd suffered renal failure while in his early fifties. "Your accident itself wasn't a life change. The life change will be the path you choose because of your gained perspective. You will know what you want from life, perhaps leaving the preaccident life behind totally."

Because of my emotional instability, he suggested my father should spend the nights with me. I agreed. I didn't feel safe in my house, not trusting AJ or the other woman if she was still in the picture. As he filled out my prescription for muscle relaxers and a schedule for three therapy sessions with his partner, Dr. M, he stated, "I'm the captain of this ship." I knew what he meant. The ship was my health care; he would guide my recovery.

Feeling rescued, I replied, "I'm glad. I'm sick of being the self-proclaimed captain of my ship for the last months. I could use a break."

NONTRADITIONAL THERAPY

AFTER SIGNING IN AT THE FROSTED WINDOW IN THE waiting room for my first appointment with Dr. M, I was escorted by one of his assistants to the back treatment room. There, he greeted me with a handshake and hug.

Dr. M was a middle-aged, short, stocky Caucasian with a personality and complexion that reminded people of Santa Claus. He asked me to sit, and then he explained that my therapy wouldn't be traditional physical therapy. "You're not a cookie-cutter case."

He said he'd couple Dr. R's prescriptions with nontraditional methods, including electrodes, chiropractic adjustments, Eastern medicine, and massages until I was ready for actual neck, back, and shoulder exercises to increase flexibility and strength. With three visits a week to start, I was a frequent flyer to that waiting room. After being called back to one of Dr. M's treatment rooms, I had many conversations with him. Strangely enough, he came to know as much about AJ and me as Virginia did. However, he always downplayed the relationship pain, probably because he hadn't been through a separation or divorce himself. Instead, he tried to reassure me about my physical rehabilitation by saying, "The muscles have been forced not to move. They are under lots of stress. They want to move."

Yet I was afraid to move them. I still wore my brace more hours a day than I didn't wear it. He understood how I needed to grow out of my fear slowly and teach my muscles to move again.

For every session, I entered through that same nondescript door, signed in at the closed window, and waited to be called to the back therapy room with its three massage-type tables. Dr. M or one of his assistants started me with heat on my shoulders and neck. Then he progressed to electrodes pulsating for fifteen minutes at different strengths from a nice, gentle pedicure-chair vibration to what I would call taser-strength zaps. After I had the first week under my belt, Dr. M asked, "Would you be okay with acupuncture?"

"I'm open to anything that gets me my body and strength back."

So he started the acupuncture, slowly and cautiously, in my hands. I expected the needles to hurt, but on the contrary, they weren't painful at all. It was a shock to see various long needles in my body aimlessly hanging on. After my first treatment, I admitted I felt the endorphins. After another few weeks, I had progressed from electrodes and acupuncture to flexibility and strength exercises. Then to break up the ever-strong knots, I received muscle massages. The staff suggested I needed to complement their efforts with home massages as well, so "masseur" was added to my father's lengthy job description.

As I commented to Dr. M, "This is more painful than what I was expecting. It's more painful now than the pre-treatment." He replied, "That's normal. You're reteaching your body to go back to what was normal. You must break the old habits and eventually get rid of the brace."

Just like a chameleon, I had to adapt.

KIDNAPPED

KIDNAPPED MAY BE THE WRONG WORD FOR MY FRIEND'S help. But that was her word for it, so I defer to her wisdom and craziness.

After I returned to Florida, my friend Karol, who takes "busy" to another level being a caregiver to all, wanted to see me and help in any way she could. Despite numerous conversations over the previous months, it was difficult to tell her the entire story. Some was history, but crucial elements were still unfolding.

When my mother returned to Massachusetts leaving my dad alone to help me, Karol wanted to step in and give me a dose of TLC. The only way she could do so involved taking charge and kidnapping me to her home in Palm Beach County.

One afternoon, she and her teenage son pulled up in my driveway and asked me to pack my things for the weekend. Although I didn't feel ready to be a houseguest, she didn't allow me to object. Hearing her contagious laugh, into the van I went, a voluntary hostage of the family.

We arrived at the house in less than an hour, which allowed me to share enough of the details of the accident and the predicted outcome. I also divulged why I was at the house alone and not with AJ.

After sharing my chaotic saga, I entered their world. Regardless of the day of the week or time of year, their house was always crazy. If it wasn't the numerous cats and dogs, it was Karol's work calls, her mother's appointments, her teenage son's sports schedule, and visits from the two older boys, one living in Florida, the other at school in Boston. I always said everyone is crazy if you know him or her well enough. And, yes, Karol's family is a bit loco but a *good* crazy.

By being kidnapped, I escaped my lonely house filled with memories of him, the past, and us. In an odd way, being in their busy, zoo-like home made me temporarily forget about my total mess.

Over the next few days, I went along with all of the scheduled and impromptu activities, including lacrosse games, landscaping, baking, board games, and walking the dogs. All the while, I got pieces of advice from just about everyone except the pets.

Karol's mother gave her two cents by doing my astro-logical reading. She said I was never well matched with AJ. She, like the Jehovah's Witness before, predicted that the end was near. Based on my zodiac sign of Sagittarius and the moons, she thought that the year of the dragon—which was six months away—would be my chariot.

Karol's husband, Will, the rock of the household, also

shared advice. His marriage prior to Karol ended in a nasty divorce that involved not only kids but a business, too. He told me, "You know, you have to know someone well before you can properly hate them. I know my ex-wife, the C U Next Tuesday (code word around the house for the four-letter word for a bitchy woman to hide from the boys until they were old enough to understand), well." I laughed. How true it was. I didn't know AJ well until my accident and recovery.

Then Will became serious and explained his personal spinal injury story. It turned out he had fractured his sixth cervical vertebra. He, too, was part of the secret cervical spine injury group. Hearing about his recovery methods and survival story helped me more than what any of my doctors told me. He was the first to suggest I start taking off the brace for sleeping. "What can you lose?" I started that evening.

Always wanting to get the last word, Karol took me outside away from the noise of video games and animals. She sat down with a glass of wine for each of us, pulled back her blond hair in a ponytail, and said, "Things will get better. You are going through one of the three worst things in life: divorce, death, and moving."

After not just a weekend but an extended four-day trip, she drove me home. "I was so happy to be kidnapped, Karol. Your place is like my Ritz Carlton. Same time same place, another week?"

"You'd better believe it!" Although Karol's version of "having it all" was not what I wanted, her family members helped me more than they will ever know. From then on, I considered them my family, too.

THE TIPPING POINT: SMOKE-FILLED HOME

USING HEAT AS DR. M ORDERED, I PURCHASED REUSABLE heating pads. After each use, to restart the pad, I needed to softly boil the plastic pouch in water on the stove. With far too many things on my mind, I ruined more than one by overcooking and melting it to the stove.

In the most memorable case, I had used a heating pad prior to both my counseling and physical therapy appointments. As scheduled, my father picked me up. He asked if I was ready. I grabbed my purse, got in the car, and replied while shutting the door, "Yep, I'm as ready as I'll ever be." However, what he failed to ask was whether I'd turned the stove off. In a situation like mine—physically needy, doped up on mood-enhancing drugs, and going through trauma, baggage, and more—I needed someone there to prevent my mistakes. My dad was just what he had always been— loving, supportive, but not a details person who would double-check to see if a stove had been left on.

We returned home after the appointments to see black smoke billowing out of the front door, smelling of burnt plastic. I immediately knew what was going on; my father was not so quick to react. The entire house, the furniture, my clothes, and everything smelled of a burnt tire like I lived next to an incinerator. I was panic-stricken.

After we hurriedly opened all of the windows and set up fans, I went into a hysterical frenzy. I worried that the house smelled, and I was having company the next day. What a reaction!

I almost burned down my house, for Christ's sake. And wouldn't that be a good ending to this saga? I had a life-threatening accident, lost my job, my husband cheated on me, and I burned down my house. It definitely was a good start to a country song—just insert a pickup truck or dead dog and a six-pack of cheap beer.

Regardless, I yelled at my dad, the one who was there helping me through this mess. "I need you to be more aware! You're treating me like I'm normal, in control, and responsible."

He responded, "How was I to guess you had left the stove on?"

I looked at him with disapproval and said, "You have to treat me as if I don't know what I'm doing!" It was true. I needed him to be more of a leader and pick up my slack.

Out of frustration, I sat down, defeated. "It's clear I'm not functioning on all four cylinders. I need help and not from another person who functions on fewer than four cylinders. I need a team of professional keepers."

After a while, we both started to laugh. What's better than laughing at your own incompetence, especially with someone else? I stupidly forgot to turn the stove off, which in turn made my house smell like an underage-drinking field party in small-town Wisconsin where people burn tires to stay warm.

It was a good thing my visitor came from such a small town.

DOSE OF FRIENDSHIP

Wɪᴛʜ ᴛʜᴇ ʜᴏᴜsᴇ sᴍᴇʟʟɪɴɢ ᴏꜰ sᴍᴏᴋᴇ, ᴍʏ ᴅᴀᴅ ʜᴇʟᴘᴇᴅ ᴍᴇ tidy up for my guest. He, of course, took out the trash after my last experience. Then, anxiously, I got into his car to ride to the airport to greet my lifelong friend Elaine.

It had been almost three years since I had seen her—a time during which she, ambitious as always, had sold her first home, purchased another, met her mate Jay, and gotten married. Regardless of the time that had passed, it wasn't hard to pick her out of the crowd with her long, beautiful brunette locks, Arizona tan, and a Colgate smile. As my dad pulled over, I got out of the car. She immediately hugged me like no time had passed, yet carefully, as I still wore my cage.

We arrived at my house and caught up on the important stuff over perfect hors d'oeuvres—carbs, cheese, more carbs, and wine. This provided fuel for our blast-from-the-past stories of high school and our college dorm room in Sellery Hall in Madison. At one point I asked, "How was your honeymoon to Australia and the Great Barrier Reef? I got your postcard. It looks amazing."

She smiled and answered, "I think you would love it. I brought pictures and videos so I can show you Australia and also the wedding. You were missed." How sad that I wasn't there! And I didn't even know her husband. I felt like a horrible friend. How could I have been absent long enough to miss the courtship, engagement, and ceremony, too?

After viewing her photos, we delved into the real emotional baggage. I went upstairs, got the letter written by the other woman, and then read its three-and-a-half pages aloud. Although I had told her on the phone only weeks before, hearing the words written by another come out of my mouth was mind-blowing. Having been through a cheating partner saga herself, she shared some of the feelings she remembered. I found that consoling. "I felt stupid, inferior, ashamed, and angry. I found out through a letter as well, but I didn't need to find it. She sent it to me via mail," she said.

Although it shouldn't have felt comforting to hear of Elaine's past pain, I was reassured as well as soothed to hear someone who was my age, not a parent or a counselor, telling me that "I've been there." Elaine admitted this letter rekindled some old feelings.

The following day, we made plans to have dinner at my house with Elaine's cousin, Stu, who was also a high school classmate of mine. It had been almost as long since I had seen him, in spite of us living in the same town. He had heard about my accident from Elaine and Facebook, but he didn't know how my recovery was going. After explaining the who, what, where, when, and how about my accident and rehab, I freely told him about my other major issue: a cheating husband. Without commenting, Stu just grabbed another bottle of wine, opened it, and poured us all another glass. It was as if the horrible story I had tortuously kept under lock and key was in free flow.

Although I was scared at first, telling my story got easier each time. Plus, the wine helped.

Shortly afterward, we heard a knock on the front door. Alarmed, I asked, "Who is it?" Then I heard my father's voice.

I opened the door and saw Adriana, my childhood friend whom I'd known since we were both farm girls with long brunette braids in kindergarten. With her now sensible, shoulder-length brown hair, she immediately dropped her bag from her swimmer's broad shoulders and hugged me without hesitation. I broke down and cried from pure surprise and happiness. Then Elaine, Adriana, and I all hugged. The three of us were together again.

I asked, "How in the world did you manage to get away?"

Adriana said with a mischievous look and smile, "I couldn't have pulled this off without your dad or Elaine. It's payback for the times you surprised me in Minnesota and in Puerto Rico for our thirtieth birthday. Right now, I'm on spring break from the university."

We retired to the kitchen island for the rest of the evening, telling stories and laughing until the wee hours. The next few days, we picked up the reminiscing at breakfast and continued the nonstop chatter and laughter until midnight. Everything was fair game for a good laugh. Boy, were past boyfriends' ears burning as skeletons of old relationships flew out of the closet that weekend.

Oh, how badly I needed a dose of both of my good friends. I was so reluctant to reach out to them for help because of my lack of energy, inability to drive, and all of my emotional mess. It turned out to be the best rehabilitation, both mentally and emotionally, I could have received.

I will be eternally grateful for their visit as well as the wisdom the time with them instilled in me. Adriana said in a handwritten farewell note, "Good friends remind us of who you were, who you are, and who you want to become." Afterward, I wondered if health insurance would cover plane tickets for friends.

What could be better than friend therapy?

PSYCHIC SLAP IN THE FACE

HAVING BEEN TO A PSYCHIC ONLY ONCE BEFORE WHEN going through a crazy spell and fighting with AJ in our early years in Boston, I didn't trust much of what they say. Why? No one goes to a psychic because he or she is sane. It's when we reach the end of our ropes and feel desperate—most likely because of love, money, or health, all of which we have little control over. And a psychic doesn't have any say or control over them either.

During Elaine's visit, she told me about her recent bachelorette party in Arizona. Instead of the stereotypical hot stripper in a police uniform, she had a psychic as entertainment. As a bachelorette party traditionalist, I would have chosen the scantily clad police officer, whipped cream, penis paraphernalia, stiff drinks, lots of dancing, and basic all-around shenanigans, but to each her own.

As a part of her psychic reading and surrounded by all of her bridal party and mutual friends of ours, Elaine asked about me, my condition, and the psychic's outlook on my recovery. She said I'd experienced a psychic slap. "Your friend was going down the wrong path. She wouldn't do it on her own. She needed a blunt hit in the head, a psychic slap."

Despite my not wanting to take a psychic's word for it, she was right.

What happened was a severe and needed wake-up call. I couldn't read the writing on the wall even when it was in bold, red, all-cap letters, and underlined to boot. The world knew I needed a change. The juggling act would cease: no more career, no more societal pressures, no more busy schedule, no more balancing friends, family, and marriage. Indeed, life had served me a dose of what I call "When All Balls Drop."

FINALLY FREE
FROM MY CAGE

I WORE MY CAGE NEARLY SIX MONTHS BEFORE IT FINALLY came off completely. And it didn't come off like a Band-Aid, quickly and painlessly. It took a few, slow months of easing my body away from its false skeleton.

I started weaning myself off the brace with only one hour to half a day until I would wear it only while riding in the car as a passenger. That was my last hurdle, as I was scared to injure the same vertebra due to a crazy Florida driver's stupidity. After encouragement and a good dose of confidence from my doctors, family members, and friends, it was time to hang my security blanket in the closet. And like the timing of nature, it was the beginning of spring. That's the day I lived my first day finally without the brace, like a butterfly carefully and slowly emerging from its cocoon.

I honored the event by spending the day with my father, Adriana, and Elaine over brunch. The company and the brunch menu brought back fond memories of Wisconsin and our childhood slumber parties. Whenever I had friends sleep over in grade school and middle school, my father made breakfast crepes—a French-style pancake—for the whole gang. Not a typical midwestern breakfast, it was a treat for all of us. He would make piles of crepes that the entourage of girls would decorate with fresh-cut apples from the local orchards, brown sugar, cinnamon, and of course maple syrup. Although he probably wouldn't admit it, he learned how to make crepes because of my mom. She made them while they were married, and after their divorce, he missed her cooking. So he took it upon himself to learn how to cook crepes.

That crepe brunch in Florida was a celebration. Not only was I in good company with good food, but I also had my freedom. Not needing the brace brought yet another step toward independence. How I wished to be completely free!

However, it wasn't the end of my physical rehabilitation or my mental and emotional healing. I still had a three-legged bar stool that was teeter-tottering.

SPILLING THE BEANS
TO STRANGERS

AFTER HIDING MY COMPLETE STORY FOR SO LONG, WHEN I finally told it, I couldn't hold back from telling the whole world.

Every chance I got, I would tell my story to anyone, including strangers such as the mail carrier. One afternoon after my appointments with Dr. M and Virginia, I heard my doorbell ring. I wasn't expecting a visitor, so I started to imagine who it could be. What bad news could he or she be bringing?

I looked through the peephole and saw the local post-woman. She had a package that required my signature. I had seen her many times over my years at the house and even more recently on my walks around the neighborhood. So I smiled and thanked her for bringing the papers. As I was signing for the delivery, I explained, "Thank you! These are legal documents to protect me from a cheating husband."

She was not surprised but rather supportive as she said,

"I'm happy to deliver these. Whatever he did to you, you don't deserve it. You deserve much better, a nice girl like you. I've had one of those cheating husbands, too. You're better off without him." I smiled gratefully, agreed, and closed the door.

That evening, I told my father about this experience. He laughed and said, "I did the same thing."

I couldn't believe it and said, "What? You talked to her, too?"

He clarified. "No, I didn't talk to the postwoman, but I did talk to a telemarketer. When your mother wanted a divorce, I needed to talk. Although I talked to friends, I once talked to a telemarketer about my divorce. I imagine he was sorry to get my number on his cold call list, but I needed to get some things off my chest, just like you did. It's normal."

GET A DOG

I HAD FOUND DR. R, STARTED ACCEPTING FRIENDS AND family visits, and went regularly to a counselor. Now it was time to talk career with my former boss, Matt.

A successful entrepreneur in his early seventies, Matt was a Wisconsinite like me. When he was growing up, his family ran a theme park in the Wisconsin Dells, a place that every Wisconsin kid, including myself, associates with summer fun. Since the Dells, Matt moved to the East Coast for college and settled in Fort Lauderdale. It was not unlike my path out of the Midwest to go east to Boston and then south to Florida.

After getting through his gatekeeper, his loyal executive assistant of multiple decades, I was able to squeeze a meeting into his schedule at the local coffee shop. It had been nearly six months since we'd spoken over the phone. I wanted to communicate to Matt in person that I was much better than in the fall. Granted, I wasn't ready to go back to work yet, but I wanted to show him I had only a little way to go, in hopes of keeping the door to my former position open.

Like most people who hadn't seen me for a while, Matt was shocked at my appearance. He complimented me on looking healthy. I guess no one can imagine what someone would look like after a thousand-pound tree limb smashes into her neck and skull. Then he asked about my next steps. Having gone through health scares himself, he said, "Sometimes the last ten yards are the hardest."

When he inquired about my husband, I was frank with him. He looked disappointed, but he shared with me that his first marriage didn't work out well either. In fact, he said it probably lasted seven years longer than it should have.

At the end of our meeting, Matt stressed putting my health on the back burner, which seemed illogical. I looked at him almost bewildered, as that was where I was spending the majority of my time and energy. To clarify what he meant, he said, "The first thing you should think of in the morning is what outfit to wear and what color eye shadow to wear, not each step and breath." He also suggested getting a dog might be a good idea.

Needless to say, I took some advice and left some.

After rethinking what Matt said, I concluded he was suggesting I needed a distraction. Although a dog was probably not the solution (I could barely take care of myself), perhaps getting out, buying a new wardrobe, and socializing would be helpful.

I, of course, shared this conversation with my family. And only a week later, when my mom came to visit again, she brought me a dog. It wasn't a real dog. It was a battery-operated dog to keep me company. When turned on, it wouldn't bark, but it would peacefully breathe as if napping. We named my dog Buddy.

Thank goodness I didn't have to feed it or walk it.

WISDOM FROM BRYAN

My Canadian colleague Bryan, a father, grandfather-to-be, francophone, and wine lover, was originally from Canada's Midwest but relocated to a remote part of British Columbia. He always reached out to me after major milestones in my recovery, whether it was leaving the hospital, returning home to Florida, or starting rehabilitation with Dr. M.

In his early sixties, Bryan had much practical advice from living through a back injury himself, as well as having ups and downs in his professional career as a lawyer. He wisely chose to chime in around those positive milestones because he knew they weren't always easy, nor were they always triumphs. I learned they could entail a hodgepodge of emotions with a few highs but with more work, pain, and stress than expected.

Bryan helped me understand a lot about my second stage of recovery, which was the physical and emotional therapy in Florida. I thought I would get stronger much faster than I did. "I can't believe how painful this is," I kept saying.

"It is pretty usual to have very brief relief followed by more pain in therapy. However, don't quit; with frequent therapy you will see results. And you need to couple this with home maintenance, too. By the way, are you meditating?"

At the time, I wasn't meditating, at least not successfully. I had purchased a meditation pillow and a couple of CDs, plus I got my dusty yoga mat out of the trunk of my Honda Accord. Although I tried meditating in my living room or bedroom with my zafu and yoga mat, or just practicing meditative breathing while on the couch, I had too much on my mind. However, I attended a yoga class weekly with other folks who had been injured in accidents or were recovering from cancer, heart disease, or other illnesses. It was called restorative yoga.

Strangely enough, I needed to have others around me in order to further silence all of the conversations going on in my head. Through that stillness, I finally let go. However, meditation was no different than physical therapy. It wasn't all rainbows and lollipops. Through deeper meditation, I cried and acknowledged my loss. Afterward I felt relief, but in the midst of meditating, it was a scary realization of both pleasure and pain.

Bryan openly shared a part of his past. He, too, had created a new path from his hurdles. Although he started as a corporate oil and gas lawyer, he changed his course by working for start-ups in the technology industry while working remotely from a secluded BC condo. He'd take the afternoons to either kayak or bake sourdough bread.

He altered his career path because of health reasons as well as knowing that corporate law wasn't a good lifestyle fit. Bryan was witty—unlike the lawyer in him—and knew how to complement our heavy conversations with a personal anecdote full of tasteful humor.

One day after hearing about the size of the evil tree, he jokingly said, "Pick smaller opponents and you'll win more often." It struck me as an ingenious way to spin the situation into something funny. Boy, did I need light-hearted conversations that weren't all about finances, health, insurance, and relationships. Thank you, Bryan!

Changing the Cocktail

During my recovery, I had a smorgasbord of prescription drugs for pain, depression, anxiety, and sleep. It started in New York with Percocets, which were not my favorite. But if you're looking to live in a dazed, numbed state and, of course, not poop for weeks, they work like a charm.

For sleeping, my first doctor prescribed an antidepressant, which didn't work at all. Limited to my cage and in constant pain, I needed a stronger heavy-duty sedative. However, knowing that my doctor would say I already had a solution that he trusted, I followed the advice of a family friend who recommended supplementing my medication with a homeopathic rose oil nicknamed LaLa Drops. Being in dire need of sleep, I tried them.

For a couple of weeks, each evening I would place two to three drops under my tongue, which would make me immediately lightheaded. I did fall asleep more quickly and slept longer, which was progress—just enough to keep me steps away from insanity's ledge.

When I returned to Florida, I needed a real sleeping drug. I couldn't get to sleep in my own bed because of my physical discomfort combined with the emotional distress of dealing with my husband and his extracurricular activities. So I made an appointment with my local general practitioner. Although I felt like a borderline psychotic when I entered his office, I put on an Oscar-winning performance of holding myself together. After all, I was in a brace, just back from four unplanned months out of my home, my marriage was in ruins, and I hadn't slept in days. With a switched cocktail, I finally slept.

When I started with my continuing-care doctor in Florida, Dr. R, I was given a tasting menu of cocktails depending on the flavor of treatment: pain or mood. He started out with muscle relaxers, which slurred my speech but certainly made the world easier—not necessarily painless but more blurred. These were paired with sleeping pills at night as well as counseling sessions multiple times a week.

When I increased my physical therapy to include stretching, resistance training, and massage, my prescription changed from the muscle relaxers to Valium and added pain relievers. This combo cocktail matched my needs better. I was going through raging emotions dealing with my husband's infidelity while also experiencing growing pains from muscles that hadn't supported my body for nearly half a year. Instead of merely slurred speech, this cocktail made me unbalanced. One evening with my dad, I fell over while kneeling, looking for a book stashed in one of the drawers of the coffee table. In falling, I bonked my forehead on the tiled floor, leaving another bump and mark on my head.

Wasn't I a trip?

After a while, I had a period of three months during which Dr. R weaned me to lower doses of Valium and zero pain meds. I did continue with the sleeping pills, as there was no way I could sleep while going through so many changes. In fact, some nights the sleeping pills didn't work either.

I simply couldn't press pause on my thoughts about betrayal and how I'd disregarded the many red flags earlier in our relationship. On nights like these, what I really needed was a horse tranquilizer or a roofie (the date rape drug) to put my mind at rest!

To my dismay, Dr. R didn't prescribe either, so I had to deal with the fog of the next day and use the combination of sheer exhaustion and a regular sleeping pill to do the job the following night.

Although it worked at the time, pill popping wasn't a long-term solution for me. I wanted to be pain free and happy *without* pills.

Fool Me Once, Shame on You; Fool Me Twice, Shame on Me

Because I trusted and loved AJ, I had overlooked so much. In retrospect, I wouldn't have put up with such things from even a gym acquaintance or a jerk at work. Because of my feelings for him, the love superseded my gut instincts. I didn't want to believe what was really going on.

My omissions in acknowledging my husband's behavior made a three-strikes-you're-out scenario look strict. I had given him so many more chances than he deserved. Most women would have left after finding the letter. But I waited, wanting to hear it for myself. Then with the accident, my recovery, and dependence on him for basic needs, he started from scratch. The tree gave him a get-out-of-jail-free card.

My accident was a way for him to repent, like the good Catholic his mother thought he was. What would most people in his situation give for one of those get-out-of-jail-free cards for living a double life? What would they have done with the opportunity? Would they have continued to cover up as he did? Or would they call it a gift?

While I was in New York and Massachusetts, AJ was a good actor—whether it was walking with me over the Hudson when I couldn't do it alone or rescuing me before the holidays. It was all for appearances' sake during a time when I needed him to be there (or foolishly believed I did).

After returning to Florida, I saw clearly the strategy he had chosen: biding his time. Later, I found out that while I was in the ER and then the ICU, he had phoned his mistress nine times. I would call that a huge sin. Not only was it continuing an adulterous relationship, but it was also downright uncaring, despicable behavior in my most critical hours.

I thought I needed the truth to heal. And I did. But I didn't comprehend that I already knew the truth. Why did I need to hear it from the source?

Honestly, it would have felt good if he'd cared enough or manned up enough to tell me in person. However, with the letter and e-mail trails and phone records, there wasn't any need for more truth to be told.

New Name: RB
for Rat Bastard

Nearly six months after reading the letter from the other woman—through countless sleepless nights, numerous meditative walks, and of course a blunt hit on the head—I decided it was time. I had to cut my ties with AJ.

Yes, admittedly I had married a con man. And I had put him on a pedestal for far too long.

I began my closure by no longer calling him by his name or his self-chosen nickname. His Brazilian birth name was always difficult for others to pronounce, but I thought it was only respectful for people to learn a name and try to say it correctly. I had always called him by his birth name. However, after falling prey to wanting to fit in in Florida and especially at college, he wanted to go by his self-chosen nickname of "AJ," which I thought was a bit juvenile. So, as a part of my resolution to wash him out of my hair, I selected a more appropriate name: RB, standing for Rat Bastard.

From that day on, I referred to him only as RB.

SCAVENGER HUNT FOR A DIVORCE LAWYER

AFTER MAKING THE DECISION TO FINALLY DIVORCE RB, how would I find a divorce lawyer?

My friends were mostly newly married or single and thus not likely to have great divorce lawyers in their Rolodex. Most of my family wasn't from the area. I couldn't just search online or open up the dusty phonebook atop the refrigerator. So I turned to my professional connections. Almost immediately, I got two contacts from my friend Patsy, who had gone through divorces herself and recently had filed most of the paperwork for her boss's divorce.

To my disbelief, I learned it would be an expensive process. Yes, like everyone else, I'd heard stories of messy and expensive divorces. However, I somehow thought mine would be different, since I was from the lower ranks of society. In reality, we had few assets to divide and more debt than anything. Without kids or businesses to split, it should have been easy.

The first lawyer's fee and retainer was $15K. How in the world can an unemployed, injured wife pay that amount? What's another option? With call number two, it would initially be half the price of $15K. But it came out to nearly $10K when all was said and done. I was disillusioned.

Then from my feelings of desperation came an "aha" moment. I should ask Virginia; she deals with these issues all day every day. At our next appointment, not only did she have a recommendation but she also assured me that her peer—whose name was Sandy—was an expert in expedited divorces. And her fees were affordable. All I heard was "fast" and "not breaking my little bank."

After leaving Virginia's office, I called Sandy immediately. I learned her fee—around $5K—would be a fraction of the cost I'd been quoted. That seemed like a steal.

So I set up an appointment with Sandy to coincide with my mother's second visit. I knew I would need emotional support even for a brief appointment. I expected it to be a difficult, painful transition. To make matters worse, my decision and the appointment with Sandy coincided with a significant milestone: our ten-year anniversary.

On the appointment day, my mother and I drove to the location—a small, single-family home turned into office space skirting a not-so-nice neighborhood with multiple drive-thru liquor stores, pawn shops, and payday loan offices. The office windows were barred with a flashing neon sign advertising bail bonds in the main front window. If I had seen a picture of the place before making the appointment, I wouldn't have gone ahead with it. I hadn't spent time in jail. I wasn't out on bond. I just needed an el cheapo divorce and *rápido*.

Despite the less-than-ideal office and unsettling surroundings, we went in. Feeling anxious, I was quickly put at
ease as Sandy described her credentials and explained how
she knew Virginia. She then asked me to share my story.

"After ten years together and almost four years married,
I need a divorce. Nearly six months ago, I found out he'd
been cheating on me with a younger woman for over a year.
Freakishly, the very next day, I broke my neck. I spent many
months in the care of my mother as well as my cheating
husband. After returning home to Florida and continuing
my recovery with both a doctor and Virginia, I am now
strong enough to make this decision. I can't continue to be
married. He will be leaving for New York in a month and a
half. I need this to be quick. "

Sandy, who had gone through divorce herself, said,
"This is a hard decision for anyone, let alone with the added
pain of your recovery. This isn't going to be easy, but I will
make it as painless as I can."

I added, "Although I've made up my mind, I haven't
told RB yet. I wanted to get all of the details first. Can we
complete this while he's here in Florida?" She said that
because of the simplicity of the case, without kids and very
few assets, the time line would be doable as long as she
could serve the paperwork shortly.

"Can you give me until after the weekend and another
session with Virginia?" I felt that I needed to talk to Virginia
to practice how I would tell RB. I was too emotionally raw
to do it alone.

"Of course."

After three days of preparing a script, talking to Virginia
and my mom, and "celebrating" our ten-year anniversary

without even sending or receiving a text, I called RB. Although I thought I was ready, when he picked up, I had to use my script almost verbatim. It was my crutch; I could have been derailed at any point.

Although I was proud of myself for having made it to the end of the script without a breakdown, stutter, or tear, I wondered why it hurt so much. It was what I wanted.

RB responded as if he'd known this conversation was coming. He smugly replied, "That's fine. This is just like you, so friendly to call me up to say I will be getting a call from your lawyer.

"I only want the car."

New Look for My Next Chapter

With spring came spring cleaning, life without the brace, and a new look.

And just in time, my reinforcement crew—my mom—came for her second visit to help with the divorce lawyer, spring cleaning, and redecorating the house. Together, not only did we paint various rooms to change the appearance from ours to mine, but we also cleansed the house by burning sage.

I was skeptical of burning *anything* after almost burning the house down with the heating pad, but she assured me it was a spiritual tradition called smudging. Although not ordinarily a spiritual person, I bought into anything that would get rid of the bad mojo from RB in the house—whether it was burning an herb or resurrecting the Ouija board of slumber parties past.

So while carrying a small bouquet of burning sage, I went through the two-story house room by room from downstairs to upstairs in a clockwise fashion. I vocalized in each room, "Make this a healthy place that I can call my home. Give it good energy." I made sure to open all closet doors and drawers to cleanse the house thoroughly and for good. Then I returned to the living room where I started and extinguished the sage into a shell. I placed the shell where RB had spent the most time: in front of the TV. As the smudging smoke dissipated and a slight aroma lingered, I felt a little silly. How could I feel better by chanting through the house with smoking sage like a shaman?

Regardless, I had taken the house back.

With the house under its new decor and recently smudged, I had another important piece of business: to get my hair done. It was the first time in almost a year I had my hair washed, cut, colored, and styled at a salon. Not having a particular hairdresser, we went to the local, high-end spa prepared with an arsenal of photo examples of cuts to show the stylist. To my unpleasant surprise, the stylist happened to be an older bald man. Not knowing this in advance and a more than little anxious, I questioned why I should trust a bald man with my hair. Who would trust a skinny pastry chef or an out-of-shape personal trainer?

I walked in, just a raw ball of emotions. More than ever before, I couldn't survive with only a subpar haircut or a bad color job. I needed a new *look*, not a new catastrophe. Please let the old adage of "don't judge a book by its cover" be right, at least *this* time.

Nearly two hours later, with auburn highlights and a fresh, cosmopolitan, fun, layered look, I stepped out of the salon smiling and confident, which was just what I needed. Finally I looked good on the outside.

Now I had only to wait for the insides to catch up to the exterior.

Remain Friends with a Douchebag? No Way

I received an unexpected call from RB only days after *the* call.

Not knowing why he'd call me, I assumed it was trouble. He said, "I thought you'd like to know that I received a call from your lawyer. I'll sign the papers on my next day off."

I was grateful he had been contacted and to know when he was planning on signing the papers. However, I was surprised he would call. I imagined my lawyer would inform me of progress, not my soon-to-be ex-husband.

At that particular moment, he sounded remorseful. "You know, I've been a real douchebag through all of this. I hope we can be friends. You have been such a large part of my life."

Shocked, in disbelief, and hurt, I couldn't believe he used the word *douchebag*. I *hated* the word; it didn't at all encompass what a complete liar, cheater, thief, and con artist that he was. On top of it all, how could I have loved a person who called himself a douchebag? What an immature way for a person in his thirties to characterize himself! Could I be friends with a douchebag? No way.

Besides, although it sounded like a comforting self-insult on his part, I knew it was a ploy to get yet another thing from me. And I was right: he needed something signed. He asked, "Could you fill out a character reference for a new apartment in New York?"

"No, I refuse to do it. You can do everything else on your own. Find a friend or employer to vet for you!"

Although I wanted him out of my life, in hindsight, I should have filled out the reference as truthfully as he deserved. Would you hire this person? No. Is this person trustworthy? Absolutely not. How would you describe the applicant? A douchebag!

CATHARTIC PHOTO SHOOT

CLOSER TO BEING HEALED, STEP BY PAINFUL STEP, WITH MY team of doctors, therapists, and lawyers, I also needed the help of a photographer.

I knew that coming back from an extended time out of work, I would need many tools from my marketing and PR past. Although I was not emotionally or physically well enough to start looking for work, network, or interview, I still had to prime the pump. I would start with a professional headshot for business cards that could also be used for a website.

So I contacted a family-run studio I'd worked with many moons before when I was an event planner for large functions. While I was making the appointment, the owner recognized my name. She remembered I had organized her son's rehearsal dinner before his wedding. I, too, remembered that event well, as the couple wed the day before RB and I did. That wasn't the first time I'd asked for her studio's photography services. Who do you think took the photos at our private beach wedding?

Needless to say, on the day of my photo shoot, the photographer and I had much catching up to do. I shared with her my traumatic story of the tree, the infidelity, the job loss, and my decision to get a divorce. She particularly identified with that as she had just gone through a divorce from her husband, the father of her sons and her business partner as well. She immediately understood what this photo shoot was about: triumph, joy, and survival.

She also knew I wasn't looking for a glamour shot or something sexy. She smiled, grabbed her two cameras, and said, "Sit back and relax. I'm going to make sure your photo communicates that you're back—better and bolder than before."

Through the multiple backdrops, outfits, poses, bright lights, and camera flashes, the photo shoot was a complete distraction from my world. I needed someone just like this photographer, a woman starting a new path, to understand what I wanted to express in my photo and then get that out of me.

I couldn't do it all on my own, but with her artful eye and postshoot airbrushing, we nailed it. I felt proud of the person I was. I was stronger than I thought. The photo exuded it, too.

LAUGHTER IS THE
BEST MEDICINE

HANDS DOWN, ALL OF MY DOCTORS AND THERAPISTS
needed to take a lesson from my friend Patsy.

Originally from Chicago, Patsy was not only well-trav-
eled, lively, and kind but also had the world's best sense of
humor. Being a wise woman with a couple of tremendous
relationship and health hurdles behind her, Patsy knew I
would need laughter to get through this mess. As my boss's
executive assistant, Patsy was one of the first people RB
had called from the hospital. It was, of course, no laughing
matter, but she had the responsibility of sharing the unfortunate news, the hospital's address, and RB's phone number
for any updates.

Once I was in Massachusetts, she stayed in contact
through instant messenger each week and sent packages
filled with entertainment. My favorite of the boatload of
boxes she sent was the complete *Cheers* series. The timeless
humor of the characters and their shenanigans kept me

company during the day when I was alone, and they helped me at night when I couldn't sleep. I thought it ironic I was recovering outside of Boston where I had met RB and lived for years, while watching a series recorded in the same surroundings.

When I returned to Florida, I didn't know how consoling it would be to share a bottle of wine and a movie with Patsy. She had never before visited my home. So I invited her in, poured her a glass of wine, and gave her a quick tour before we sat on my couch to finally catch up. As I told her about RB, she was not surprised by the lies and lack of creativity in his cover-ups. Then I listened to her stories of not one but two failed marriages. Like little kids, we swapped stories like stickers. How we laughed not only at our own stupidity but at the stupidity of our dumb exes!

We were so busy telling stories that we neglected to watch the movie. However, we didn't make the same mistake with the wine.

On another occasion, I visited Patsy's condo also for the first time. It was small but every square inch was eclectically decorated with furniture from Korea, images from Australia and the South Pacific, and family heirlooms. I was inspired by her travel souvenirs and photos, especially Ayers Rock, Thailand, and the South Pacific's tropical beaches. I knew from that night I wanted to take a walkabout to see the world with my new eyes. Patsy's humorous travel tales and beautiful adventures reinforced my need to become as vivacious as I was before, if not more so.

I needed to see the world. Perhaps in doing so, I would stumble upon love again—this time with a partner I could trust.

CREATING A HOLIDAY: LOOK UP DAY

HOW COULD I PAY RESPECT TO THE MANY LESSONS OF MY accident and recovery?

I knew all too well my old habits would try to take over. It would be easy to jump into the same routine and follow society's unwritten rules of working too hard, playing too little, and not appreciating the most important things in life: health, friends and family, and freedom.

I thought celebrating a yearly anniversary wasn't enough and daily would be too much. However, I decided that a monthly observance would be just right. To coincide with the date of the accident, September 27, I made the twenty-seventh day of each month a special holiday. When I asked my peers and connections for a name for the twenty-seventh, I got a laundry list of possible names. Many were religious, others in foreign languages, and some dealt with the theme of rebirth or a second birthday. I steered away from those to find something more creative yet still encompassing the meaning of my many lessons.

When I received this suggestion from a travel peer, I knew it was spot on: Look Up Day. It perfectly conveyed the double entendre of being aware of our surroundings and spinning each situation in a positive way. Look Up Day would remind us to look up for both beauty and hazards while turning our current circumstances into opportunities.

Thanks for the idea, Kris. Here's to looking up!

THE JOY OF
DRIVING AGAIN

I HAD NEVER ENJOYED DRIVING. AND LIKE MOST WIVES, I typically took the passenger seat. But over the previous six months of waiting for rides, asking for favors, and always being the needy passenger, I would have paid a high price to drive myself away from my various house arrests spanning from New York to Massachusetts to Florida.

In fact, I never understood what a privilege it was to drive until my recovery. How I wished I could have gotten into a car and driven when I didn't get answers from RB or even when the unwelcome mat hit me in the ass!

After being carted around by my dad and friends in Florida for nearly two full months, I finally started to drive again. Just like when I was a teenager, my dad was at my side in the passenger seat. We began with short, one-mile drives from the house to the grocery store. To make things easier for me and my neck, we would leave the car parked in the driveway instead of the garage. This made backing up only a minor obstacle instead of a grand feat. I did the same with parking lots, choosing the farthest spot away from the store with no cars on either side so I could make an easy exit.

Then we progressed to driving to the doctor's office, a five-mile drive. I didn't attempt anything in rush hour or on highways for quite some time. It was scary. South Florida has been known for some of the worst driving in the country, including hit and runs, pedestrian strikes, and of course Spanglish road rage—*Estúpido, watch the road! Carajo!*

How ironic for Dad to teach me how to drive again. He originally taught me on a 1976 Ford automatic truck in the pasture of our Wisconsin hobby farm. Then we progressed to the local country roads zigzagging through valley after valley into town before hitting the highway. Afterward, he insisted I learn how to drive a stick shift, which came in handy when renting cars in Mexico and Spain. In fact, when we were teenagers, I even taught one of my good friends, Elaine, how to drive a stick on an out-of-the-way country road. Almost twenty years later, she shocked me by remembering our lesson. By driving me around on her visit during my recovery, she paid me back.

Although I was fearful and a little tentative, it was wonderful to have that power of the stick in my hands. I could also control the radio station, changing from my favorite top 40 station to a little Latin salsa. Although the lack of flexibility in my neck made driving difficult, I made do with adjustments—as I'd done with all of the hurdles of the process. In this case, I had to use the mirrors a lot more than before. I also planned my route, lane, and parking space accordingly. And more than ever before, I became a defensive driver.

Driving became another step toward gaining my independence, the freedom to leave and come back when I wanted. One step at a time, I would get my liberties back. Driving: check. What would be next?

A Cheatee's Wisdom

It so happened I was experiencing what many on the global media stage were going through at the same time.

Because of John Edwards, Tiger Woods, and numerous others, I got to relive my marital problems and RB's infidelity on every medium. I couldn't escape even if I wanted to. I could have traveled to the bush of Alaska to get some peace and quiet from all of the adulterers, but most likely there would be no escape even there. Cheating was a global phenomenon. Although I could be proven wrong, I began to believe the only way a man could multitask was a ménage à trois. *C'est la vie!*

After further analyzing the shitstorm of affairs in the press as well as my own embarrassment, I came away with an arsenal of wisdom.

First and foremost, all couples have problems, but not all couples have affairs. In our case, RB made the decision to cheat. In fact, his father cheated, too. That's why I never met him in Brazil. I should've known that the apple didn't fall far from the tree. However, I eventually understood that neither my husband's actions nor his DNA defined me.

Second, people often blame the cheatee for being controlling. I, along with the plethora of other cheatees, beg to differ. I did not use my powerful persuasive skills to make him have an affair with a twenty-something colleague. Please. I couldn't even get him to cook at home—and he was a chef.

And last, let me address the assumption that the person who had the affair wasn't getting enough loving, attention, or whoopee at home. That's one of the reasons most of us who have been cheatees don't tell anyone at first. Who would want to be known as the frigid wife? However, it seems to be the first thing the cheater uses as bait to get the other woman's attention. The line: "Our sex life is dead."

Lots of water went under the bridge and over the dam before I found the courage to share the facts of my situation. Why? Because I couldn't deal with the scrutiny about what was wrong with *me*. I could hear the gossipers: Was she a controlling, crazy wife? Was she cold in bed and making whoopee only on birthdays and anniversaries?

I am no Dr. Ruth or Dr. Phil, but my knowledge has come straight from the trenches. Use my crib notes wisely.

Come Lie on
My Couch and
Let's Exchange
War Stories

I SOON REALIZED I HAD BECOME LIKE MY FIRST THERAPISTS: Oprah, Jerry Springer, and David Sedaris.

With my soap opera–like story filled with love, lies, accidents, pain, and tears, just about anyone in contact with me started to reveal his or her troubles. People *knew* I'd understand where they were coming from. And you bet I did. My couch was more discreet than a national broadcast and certainly more comfortable than my OB-GYN confessional, so I listened to the countless painful tales of cheaters past.

Only after I shared my RB story did my Brazilian friend, Vila, reveal her beliefs about Brazilian men. "I would never date or marry a Brazilian man just because of what I witnessed my uncles, cousins, and other men put my aunts, sisters, and other women through." I had known Vila nearly five years when she divulged her distrust of *brasileiros*. When she and I met, I was already engaged to RB. And, I had asked her for help with my Portuguese vows for our wedding. How I wished she had shared the truth of her culture earlier. But would I have listened?

Time and time again, it seemed the majority of women who had lived and survived a cheating partner were open to having a relationship again. But these women were certainly not eternal optimists. A European colleague of mine shockingly shared with me via Facebook details about a physical injury as well as adultery during her midthirties. She said, "Never expect men to rise to your expectations."

As the cherry on top, I received a call from Elaine's brother, Ed, an old friend and my quasi-brother from Wisconsin. He happened to find himself in the same boat as me—the victim of a cheating spouse. Like my female friends, he and I exchanged our war stories. I told him about uncovering the confession letter and all of the lies that had unraveled since, including finding the phone calls to the other woman when I was in the hospital. Ed commented, "Wow, that's low. They deserve each other."

Likewise, Ed shared stories of his investigation in full swing: breaking into e-mail accounts, checking phone records, and even showing up at the other man's house. We concluded the majority of the stories we knew or had experienced firsthand lacked a lot of creativity. Couldn't they have come up with better lies or cover-ups?

The best quote from the hours of conversation was a twist on the common saying "Some things you can't fix."

While we were discussing repeated infidelity, Ed laughed and said, "Some things you can't unfuck."

Although vulgar, it's true. Adultery is a hard nail to get out the coffin of a relationship or, better said, a screw to unscrew.

PAIN IN THE NECK FOR BOTH

After my mother brought me to Florida and returned to Massachusetts, she had passed the primary caregiver role to my father.

Although both my parents were there for me throughout the long haul, each took the lead at certain periods for appointments, driving, bathing, cooking, shopping, and massages. Once I miraculously found Dr. R in Florida for my continued care, I somehow gave my neck, back, and shoulder pain to my dad as well. Who would have thought my symptoms would be contagious, but they were: sympathy pains.

After a month of my treatment with exercises, electrodes, and massages, my father began having a stiff neck to the point he couldn't turn his head or reduce the pain with ice, heat, or pain relievers. I suggested he make an appointment with Dr. R since he was taking me there anyway. He reluctantly did so. I was relieved, as it wasn't any good for my chauffeur to be driving me around in pain and without the ability to turn his neck. Our situation was turning out to be the blind leading the blind.

At the next appointment, I was in the treatment room with electrodes hooked up to my back and shoulders with my father beside me on the very next machine and table— like a bizarre, warped, couples massage. His treatment was similar to mine but without the acupuncture, Novocaine, and massages. We were probably known by the staff as the not-so-powerful duo of pains in the neck.

After we had returned to our respective homes from our joint appointments, we would use the heating pads, trying not to burn either of our homes down as I had almost done. As happens with most sympathy pain, his neck got better when my pain lessened.

WEDDING SONG ON DIVORCE EVE

WHILE WAITING AT A NEWLY OPENED LAS OLAS RESTAU-
rant for four of my friends, I sat surrounded by a men's
business networking cocktail hour and ordered a drink.

Was it a sign that, the night before my divorce, I was the
only woman in the bar?

After enjoying the first sip of my drink, the band started
playing "Just the Two of Us"—our wedding song. Here I
was, about to get divorced the next day and surrounded by
an entire bar full of men. Could you believe that none of
them offered to buy me a drink?

What the hell was going on? In Fort Lauderdale or just
about anywhere, no woman in her early thirties, alone,
needs to buy her own drink in a bar when there's a room
full of guys. I felt like I was on a twisted blind date. The
combination of my impending divorce in less than twelve
hours, our wedding song from only four years earlier, and

the sheer awkwardness of being ignored by a group of forty men drove me to order another drink.

Almost as if timed, the band took a break. The organizer of the group, a well-dressed man in Florida business casual, took the microphone and thanked everyone for coming to this gay-friendly business networking event. That was my light bulb moment.

I looked down at the bar, shook my head, and bashfully laughed. I was so engrossed in my own drama that I didn't even come up with a possible secondary scenario about why no one came to talk to me or buy me a drink. Most women probably would have been refreshed by this occurrence, but I was bewildered.

Thank goodness my friends arrived. We had a good laugh at my stupidity.

No One Gets Married
to Get Divorced

Irritable and up at the crack of dawn, I stared at my closet. What should I wear to court to divorce RB?

I decided to mask any insecurity with a spiffy pencil skirt, silk top, and take-no-prisoners heels. My dad and loyal chauffeur drove me to the courthouse as I was too nervous to drive. Although I didn't think RB would appear as it wasn't mandatory, I was on guard looking for him and his silver Honda.

After finding the hearing room, we waited—not unlike much of my medical recovery. To pass the time, I started surveying those around me, just as I had done while waiting in the first doctor's office in Poughkeepsie. I wondered why all the others were in the room. Were they all family law cases or was I hanging out among thieves, assailants, or murderers?

Within a half hour, Sandy arrived, happy to see I wasn't in tears. "I never know what I'm going to show up to at the courthouse. You look good." She smiled. Then she prepped me for the questions that would be asked inside. I was grateful, as I didn't feel I was capable of good impromptu answers on such a sad day—the end of a huge chapter of my life.

Then came a wait that seemed like years. Each time a name was called, I felt hopeful but once again disappointed because it wasn't my case. Finally that day, my D-Day, I heard my hyphenated married name called (albeit horribly pronounced) for the very last time. We all entered the room, which I assumed would be a courtroom but instead was the judge's chambers. The judge, a Germanic, stoic, and no-frills woman, started the hearing matter-of-factly. Most of her questions were about assets and children. After I said we had no children, she asked, "Is there a remote possibility you could be pregnant now?"

It was a completely warranted question. After all, she didn't know about my accident and all the rest. Regardless, I let out a little laugh, thinking that, under the circumstances, it would have been an immaculate conception.

It had been well beyond nine months since I had last had sex with RB. We had not been intimate after the accident for many reasons. Heck, there were enough reasons to make anyone celibate: my pain, the brace, and his lies. I paused, collected myself, and said, "No, no way."

Her final question was about my legal name and what I would like it to be. Within another five minutes in her chambers and forty-five minutes of waiting in line for the official paperwork, I had the same legal name as when I was born. Joyously, I took another big step toward my independence.

DETECTIVE DIANA

Diana, a savvy yet coy brunette in her midtwenties, always had a plan up her sleeve.

She and I had known each other only a year when the accident happened. Over that short time, we had grown close because we traveled together for work to London, Orlando, and Los Angeles. Like any stressful environment, such as working at a busy restaurant, competing in sports, or meeting time-sensitive deadlines, travel quickly brings people closer.

Through my recovery, Diana surprised me with unusual ways of support. However, these were no "coinkidinks." She had gone through a horrible car accident in her early twenties while away at college in Texas with her family in Florida. She knew what I needed without asking and understood the recovery process firsthand.

Although Diana had been a supportive friend with thoughtful care packages and witty texts throughout my time in New York and Massachusetts, she was an even greater emotional crutch for me in Florida. When I'd shared information about RB's infidelity, she threw herself into a secret mission. She had wanted to find dirt on the other woman and RB to help me decide—one way or the other—whether to divorce or stay with him.

I considered myself an excellent investigator on the Internet at the time, but after seeing the results of Diana's search, she won. Diana was ruthless. I wouldn't want to be the target of her next investigation. She found hard evidence and got colorful social media messages from the other woman. As her way to help, she wanted to expose as much truth as possible. And what she found were photos documenting the other woman's visit to Poughkeepsie. That cleared up many of the holes in RB's lies.

So naturally after my divorce, it was only fitting to go out to dinner with my lead investigator. We didn't organize it as a celebration but rather as two friends getting together for dinner. However, it morphed into a divorce party. We chose a restaurant at the local Hard Rock casino over-looking a large lake and fountains. From our waitress, we learned that a man planned to propose to his girlfriend on the veranda via a message written in the illuminated sign when the fountain show began.

All three of us had an initial response: "Don't do it!"

I quickly explained, "I've been divorced for eight days."

The waitress congratulated me and said, "I've been divorced for eight *years*."

Within moments, she returned with a complimentary bottle of champagne for Diana and me; thus, our dinner became a divorce party. I guess it took one to know one.

After going through a divorce, even if it's something

desirable, we experience a cement mixer of heavy emotions of loss, anger, fear, and also relief and happiness. So although we didn't set the world on fire with all the grannies and veteran penny slot players that evening, it was a perfect hybrid occasion. I needed to honor both my losses and my gains from the divorce.

I hoped neither the waitress nor I tainted Diana forever on marriage.

GETTING ON
WITH BUSINESS

EAGER TO GET RID OF RB'S NAME, I DIDN'T WASTE ANY time getting my paperwork, license, and passport back to my maiden name.

My first stop was one of South Florida's Registries of Motor Vehicles (RMV), a real dose of local culture with all kinds of ugly, unhappy, impatient, and unsanitary patrons. After arriving bright and early, I stood in line outside among the masses in the already-humid, eighty-degree heat—only to find out after nearly two hours I needed more than the divorce decree and my old license. The RMV required either my birth certificate, which was at home, or a new Social Security card with my maiden name as my old card had my married name. I chose to kill two birds with one stone by going to the local Social Security office, about twenty miles across the county, to get a new card. Then I returned to the RMV and stood in the same line in the same heat for over three hours.

While waiting with all of the others who were equally as pissed, sweaty, and ripe for the picking, I thought this was the worst RMV experience ever. It even topped my first experience in Onalaska, Wisconsin, where I flunked my driving test at sixteen. How mortifying this failure was for an overachieving only child, but so was any day at the RMV anywhere. The whole RMV set-up seemed like purgatory.

However, I couldn't give up. On that day, I did what any woman would do to remove her ex's name, a blatant reminder that he'd had a hold on her existence. I refused to leave without my own name. I couldn't live another day with that awful, hyphenated, five-minute signature. After testing my patience and sanity throughout a full day of waiting at not one but two government offices, I finally left with a new license and Social Security card in my birth name.

Why in the world did I change my name in the first place? Never again. No exceptions. Not even royalty, a celebrity, or a Kennedy!

LAST WORDS

ONLY A DAY BEFORE LEAVING FLORIDA FOR SCHOOL IN New York, RB contacted me to get the title of the silver Honda. We agreed on a time for the exchange at the house, but as in every other encounter, he—the con man—wanted something extra, illegal, or just too much. He said, "I have to leave the plates on the car to drive to New York. I don't have time to get them here. When I get there, I'll get New York plates."

Hearing that, I freaked out. I just wanted to be done with it all. And I couldn't deal with yet another fight. So I said, "Fine. Take the car with the plates and be gone."

When I told my father, he was outraged. "I will be at your house when he comes to get the title. I refuse to let you give him the title without receiving the plates."

I couldn't fight with RB anymore, so I told my father, "Then you'll have to talk to him. I can't do it anymore. I don't want to see him." I stayed inside the house when RB arrived. Sitting on a couch close enough to hear the car pull up, I cried. I couldn't believe that after ten years, I couldn't even confront him over such a trivial item.

My father resolved the issue, which was basically RB's giving up the plates regardless of what he wanted. Dad wouldn't bend. Then he called RB a liar, a cheating SOB, and some other choice words. As RB was driving away, he phoned me and shouted, "You are lucky I didn't knock your father out. After today, I don't want to be insulted anymore. This is the last time. I don't want to be friends." Then he hung up.

That was it, the end. Such a large part of my life was over. His words during many fights over the years—"Heidi, I'm never good enough for you"—rang through my head over and over. I finally realized he was right.

Yes, RB, you are 100 percent right. You are not good enough! You are a douchebag!

Becoming a Godmother

Unexpected phone calls or knocks on the door after a year like I had typically meant bad news.

Only days after RB left to New York with the car, my cell phone rang in the middle of the afternoon. I was shocked to see it was a call from Ariel, a former employee of mine in her early twenties who was about to be a mom. Without much chitchat, she popped a question I certainly wasn't expecting: "Will you be the godmother of our child?"

Unable to take more than a moment to pause, I thought of all the reasons why I wouldn't be a good candidate for godmother. First and foremost, I wasn't religious. Second, I had barely been able to take care of myself over the last year. Third, I was unemployed and recently divorced.

She took my pause as an opening to explain why she selected me, saying, "I look up to you. I have a small family and group of friends who wouldn't take the responsibility. I trust you fully. That's why I'd like you to be the godmother for my unborn daughter."

I protested. "But I can't be the traditional role model for your daughter's spiritual guidance." Maybe she didn't know that I rarely went to church. In fact, I had not been to church since a friend's wedding years before. I continued to explain that there was, however, a second role of godmother I'd be willing to fulfill. I would be the support needed if life threw her a real nasty curveball: loss of home, divorce, accident, or life.

Amazing! After my near-death accident, divorce, loss of job, and overall mess, Ariel asked me to be responsible for another human being. Why? I was just barely putting myself back together. Regardless, I told her, "I'm honored to be her godmother."

I hoped I would do right by her request.

A CHARDONNAY LUNCH

As a young professional in South Florida, I had gone out for business lunches and seen the trophy wives enjoying a light lunch and drinking chardonnay with similarly entitled females. I'd looked upon them enviously as I went back to my corner office or to one of my lesser jobs in the cubicle section. However, when in Rome, do as the Romans do. Since I was in South Florida, I had to try it once.

I suggested to my friend Vila that we have a chardonnay lunch at the most happening new joint in Fort Lauderdale, owned by a former employer of ours. Everyone went there to be seen, strutting his or her stuff from exotic cars to jewelry and perhaps a new nip or tuck. As a surprise to me, Rose, a sophisticated yet down-to-earth businesswoman, joined us for lunch. I hadn't seen Rose since we had worked together on various high-end projects and events well before my accident. She learned of and kept up with my recovery through social media, but she and I were never close enough friends to phone one another; rather, we were simply professional connections.

So my dream chardonnay lunch turned out to be quite revealing. Perhaps it was Vila who knew a bit more of Rose's past than I. Otherwise, why would she surprise me by asking Rose to join us?

During our lunch, I learned of Rose's amazing past. It was shocking to hear how similar some of her history was to my recovery. She'd been in a bad car accident the summer before her senior year of high school in California. She recovered slowly, but then pushed her education and career into high gear, graduating high school early and directly entering the work world at a bank. After marrying, she sadly learned that she couldn't have children. Although disappointed, she continued making her mark by concentrating on her career and marriage while being a supportive aunt and role model for others' children.

Rose told me that in her twenties she worked so hard, she didn't have a life. In her thirties, she changed her ways to have more fun. Then in her forties, she combined working for a bank with volunteering for community projects, which gave her more freedom. At the time of our lunch, she was in her fifties working for herself and doing what she loved. After decades, she had finally found the right recipe for freedom and fun in her career.

I listened to Rose's story and related her life events to my recent accident, my previous years of climbing the corporate ladder, and the career path and lifestyle I wanted. I knew that Vila was internalizing the conversation, equating it to being in her early thirties, happily married, mother of one, and still working full-time for someone in a stressful, sixty-hour-a-week management job.

This wasn't the kiss-kiss chardonnay lunch I expected. It turned into another lesson about coping with serious injuries and health scares. Those hurdles, albeit painful, are what make life. Yes, they're hard, but they pass. The person changes not necessarily because of the event itself but because of the *knowledge* gained from it. Through these experiences, perspective is gained, often tweaking one's course.

My course was altered by adding a sense of fun and freedom, vowing to never skip a chardonnay lunch with my clan. My GPS was set on happiness.

GETTING MY CAREER LEG ON THE GROUND

With my three-legged bar stool still wobbly, I wanted to eventually get all three of its legs on the ground.

As my health, both mental and physical, was getting better and my relationships steadily supporting me now that RB had been banished, I had to think about what I'd do professionally. Wouldn't it be easier to get my old job back than to start afresh?

I reached out to my professional connections for job leads and asked their opinions about options. Two of my former supervisors strongly advised me not to try to go back to the same job. Both described that being in my old position would be like treading water: hard work to keep afloat in a business that might not succeed. My former boss asked, "Would you be happy going back to a pity position and only part-time?" Although it didn't seem appealing, it sounded better than being out of work for nearly a year. So, I needed to see it for myself.

It had been over three months since I visited my former office to gather my things. So before Memorial Day weekend, I went back again to see Beth in human resources. I had to update the team about my progress, my recovery timeline, and my long-term disability.

However, the offices looked much different; in fact, they looked dismal. Much of the staff I knew wasn't there at the time or was no longer employed. The majority of the lights were turned off. I noticed that all of the furniture and belongings had Post-its: to sell or to move. Through Beth, I learned they'd be downsizing the office space, selling nonessential furniture and supplies, and moving across town.

It was another revelation; in less than nine months, my job didn't exist anymore. It had vanished because the company was no longer looking to grow. It had to stay chugging along with residual income while decreasing its staff and other bottom-line costs. They were cutting the fat and would be happy to take home a small profit—a million or two.

Although it was another disappointment and a door closed, this visit provided yet another lesson. With the career leg of my three-legged bar stool incomplete, I had to rebuild it practically from scratch. I started to apply for positions in the area, practiced my thirty-second pitch, and began networking. I was fearful I would blabber about the not-so-appealing qualities of recovering from an accident and being recently divorced. The dreaded interview question played over and over in my head: "What have you been doing for the last nine months?" I tried to creatively spin a response, but it was empty and fake. Was being brutally honest the best bet? I broke my neck in a freak tree accident in New York, lived out of a suitcase for nearly four months, was forced to leave my job, returned to Florida for physical therapy, and divorced a cheating husband. What a résumé.

Regardless of my apprehension, I started to get my act together. I had already begun working to make myself hirable with a professional photo, business cards, and a website based on my past success in travel and technology. But I faced one minor hiccup; I didn't know what I wanted to do. I had an opportunity to completely recreate myself, but into what? I certainly knew what I *didn't* want to be from my past careers as a high school Spanish teacher, catering manager, marketing and events coordinator, and so on.

So because I didn't know what to do, I concentrated on piggybacking on my most recent job in marketing and PR. Still, a part of me wanted to do my own thing—maybe like Rose, having more fun and freedom, working for myself, and doing what I love.

That thought excited me!

Unexpected Confirmation, Not from a Fortune Cookie

Having Chinese food with my friend Chrissie gave me yet another confirmation I was on the right path. I wasn't the only professional woman who'd been duped by a con artist. Neither was I alone in recovering from an injury and hoping to regain my physical strength. We all needed time.

Chrissie was a social butterfly I'd met working in Fort Lauderdale right after I'd married RB. A high-octane young Latina a tad younger than me, she wanted to climb the professional ladder from office manager to finance and project management in global corporations. Since leaving the employer we shared at that time, both she and I had scored high-level management positions in different fields and companies. We remained in the area and stayed in touch, primarily through Facebook.

I originally reached out to her for networking in hopes of helping my job search. When she responded, I suggested having dinner on Look Up Day.

After getting a table and hot sake, we found out that, uncannily, we shared staggering similarities. She too had suffered a physical injury almost eight months before. She'd broken her leg, which made doing routine tasks as well as driving impossible for months. At the time, she was in a bad long-term relationship with a macho Miami-based model. Under his manipulative spell, she naturally leaned on her partner during her injury and recovery; he was her crutch. With time, she too recovered physically, progressing from crutches to walking and then driving and returning to work. Through this progression, she saw reality more clearly as she regained her independence little by little. She only fully felt free after suffering through many fights and break ups. She eventually severed ties and moved out.

Was I looking into a mirror?

Chrissie and I continued to compare notes as the waiter brought our food and kept the sake hot. How could this be true? I was seeing two women who'd put great pressure on themselves to succeed professionally while allowing the emotional side of their lives to be subpar, if not abusive.

Why was the woman always the caregiver or subordinate? I didn't think it had to be that way. Why was having it all—health, love, and career—so difficult?

Yes, I thought I had it all, but it was an illusion at the time. Did I need to reevaluate what all of those goals meant? Having it all was not a status, title, or address. Rather, it was something distinct to each of us, and it changed with time. I needed to redefine my having it all.

The confirmation I received that evening didn't come from a fortune cookie.

CREATING A MEMORIAL

IT WAS MEMORIAL DAY WEEKEND. IN MANY HOMES, THAT meant a long, three-day weekend filled with kick-off summer barbecues, family picnics, and camping trips or jaunts to the beach. However, I was single without many single friends and with a small family of one in the area. Everyone I knew was escaping town for the weekend with family or significant others, leaving me on a long weekend without plans.

This was the first time I realized that, when you're single, holidays can be extremely lonely. In the whole scheme of things, Memorial Day isn't on the top of the totem pole of holidays. But for me, it was a foreshadowing of what Labor Day, Columbus Day, and all of the other holidays might look like. Couples and families would leave poor single people like me to watch bad television, order take-out, and sulk on the couch.

So I decided I needed a project—to put together an album or memorial of my last nine months in pictures.

I had camera cards of photos to be developed from days before the accident, through my stays in Massachusetts, New York, and at home in Florida. I thought this project would keep my mind off of being alone.

What a horribly bad idea! It didn't keep my mind off of any of it. In fact, it made me feel worse, more alone, and sadder than ever. The process showed me in slow motion, picture by painful picture, what I had been and what I had sacrificed. It revealed the hard truth of all that had happened to me. RB was in many of the pictures, but his vacant expression showed that he wasn't really there.

Likewise, I saw myself in photos from the hospital and earlier on in Massachusetts. I was trying so hard to be strong and smile in spite of the physical pain and emotional mess. It hurt seeing the past from my new perspective.

How did I let it all happen? I certainly didn't see it unfolding, but someone, my friends or family, must have. Why didn't those around me tell me? Was I so hard-headed that, if they had told me, I wouldn't have been ready to hear it? Why did RB stay with me if he wanted someone else?

And could there have been a better messenger than a blunt hit to the head—one that let all the balls drop?

SWEAT, TEARS,
AND THE SEA

"THE CURE FOR ANYTHING IS SALTWATER: SWEAT, TEARS, and the sea," wrote Karen Blixen, author of *Out of Africa*. And that was exactly what I sought.

Preoccupied with all the recent changes and nervous about an upcoming trip back to Poughkeepsie for a deposition about the accident, I not only took Blixen's advice but also a lesson from my father's beach-bum lifestyle. I went to the beach.

Little did I know that letting all the other stuff pause for a Sunday was what I needed. There, I met Chrissie, a group of her mid-twenty-something friends, and what seemed to be the rest of South Florida. The beach was crowded with umbrellas, tents, chairs, coolers, and stereos galore, not to mention the hordes frolicking in the water.

I sat down on my towel, opened a cold beer, and joined in the fun. I felt like I was turning twenty-one again. And if being surrounded by a group of recent college graduates with techno music playing in the background wasn't enough to flash back to my UW-Madison undergrad years, I then was offered a beer bong—yes, chugging a beer through a funnel and hose. Unlike most Badgers, I didn't do beer bongs while in Madison. Why do one at thirty-three? Why in Fort Lauderdale?

Well, that day, I threw caution to the wind and said, "Why not?" Although it wasn't the best performance of chugging beer by a Wisconsinite or Badger to date, I survived, got a small round of applause, and headed to the water for girl talk.

Immediately the girls wanted to know if I was single or seeing someone, where I was from, where I lived, and the like. Chrissie told the story of how she and I had met through work years back. I then explained my background with the climax of being recently divorced from a cheating con man named RB from Brazil. Unknown to me, one of the girls was from Brazil. However, she, as well as some others from Peru, recognized my story. In fact, one of the women said, "I've been hurt, too" and toasted surviving bad relationships. We continued the afternoon exchanging war stories and laughing at our past relationship faux pas.

With a little sweat, seawater, and tears over beers, I was happy to escape the turmoil so I could slow down and regroup. I should have known that my dad had always been right with his own secret recipe for happiness: sun, beach, and margaritas with salt.

PILGRIMAGE TO POUGHKEEPSIE

AFTER A FLIGHT TO BOSTON TO MEET MY MOM, SHE DROVE us on the oh-so-familiar route from Massachusetts to the Hudson River Valley. From her home, we took the nearly two-hundred-mile drive that she and I had made many times driving through fall colors and past icy, barren fields.

With the Berkshires now lush and green, the drive was unlike the previous fall and winter. And I looked dramatically different as well. I was no longer in a brace, beaten and bruised. I'd been another person traveling through that freezing cold and injured to the core. Now, it was summer with the valley's hills in bloom and the river running. The Culinary Institute and Vassar students were out enjoying the sun on the lawns, playing Frisbee, picnicking, and studying for finals.

Although the official goal of the trip was to meet with my lawyer for a deposition regarding the accident, I also had a personal pilgrimage. Not only did I want to revisit where the accident took place and see if the evil tree was still there, I also wanted to walk or even run across the Walkway Over the Hudson. It had been my meditation labyrinth for many bitterly cold and trying months.

In Poughkeepsie, we checked in at the hotel where my mom had stayed during my recovery in the hospital and follow-up doctor's appointments. Just like her previous stays, the hotel and its predominantly Indian staff had generously honored an extended-stay, discounted rate for family members of patients at St. Francis. It certainly wasn't the Ritz-Carlton, but it had the basics: beds, hot showers, breakfast, and parking.

It was an odd combination of standard, economy hotel with an adjoining unsuccessful comedy club. It sat just off the main drag, Route 9, adjacent to a strip mall, only minutes from Main Street Poughkeepsie and St. Francis Hospital.

As we took our bags from the car and entered our room, Mom was instantly reminded of what we both had gone through. "Heidi, look at how far you have come since my last stay here. You have triumphed against many odds. Let's get something to eat to celebrate. Your choice."

I picked a Hyde Park restaurant well known for its innovative menu and open kitchen. We sat at the counter watching the chefs in action preparing our assortment of tapas. Although I remember a tasty meal and great service, it was the dessert that was unforgettable: crispy bacon dipped in dark chocolate—a first for both of us. And it just showed that everything is better with bacon—yes, even chocolate.

After traveling nearly eight straight hours from South Florida to Boston and to the Hudson River Valley, then eating a filling dinner, I was spent. We returned to the hotel hoping for a good night's sleep. However, since my arrival to the Hudson River Valley, I couldn't get rid of an overarching feeling of doom. Just being in the same county with RB was unnerving. Would I run into him? I was on high alert for that silver Honda Accord again.

It was yet another sleepless night in Poughkeepsie.

THE APATHETIC INTERVIEW

THE FOLLOWING MORNING, MY MOTHER DROVE US TO MY lawyer's office close to the Hudson River's banks.

Although I had met this lawyer in person before, it was early in my recovery when I was barely out of surgery, and I didn't recognize him. I had somehow imagined him short, but in fact he was tall and thin with brown hair and an odd, occasional facial tick. How strange to have trusted him throughout this process and be able to pinpoint his voice from all of our calls. Yet if it weren't for my mother or being at his office, I couldn't have recognized him.

He reassured me I didn't have to respond to any questions I felt I couldn't answer. Then he looked me in the eye and said, "I will be by your side the whole time. I know this is hard." Afterward, we all headed to the other lawyer's office conveniently located in downtown Poughkeepsie, only blocks from where the accident occurred. My lawyer drove his car and we followed in ours.

We entered the law office for the deposition and were

escorted to the nondescript conference room. Everything felt artificial, including the lighting, plants, and furniture. If I hadn't known any better, I would have thought I was back in my stark, square hospital room.

After waiting awhile for the other lawyer and stenographer, we began the two-hour questioning.

The opposing lawyer, a middle-aged Caucasian male with glasses, was cold and pragmatic. In a series of dozens of questions, he asked me to outline the day of the accident: where I had been, what the weather was like, and where my husband was when the accident occurred. I was on edge, but I tried to answer succinctly. Up to that point, no one had listened to my story with such apathy. Clearly, he was going through the facts of the story only for the purposes of the recorded deposition. He wanted to see if he could find any holes in my story or my character. He looked for any reason to believe it wasn't the tree that had caused my accident.

The accident details, lists of my medications, and doctors both in Florida and New York were rather easy for me to recite; I had done it countless times. However, when he started to ask about my marriage and the divorce, those personal questions seemed invasive. He asked about the length of my marriage, if it was abusive, and if the accident caused the divorce. Trying unsuccessfully to remain composed, with my voice shaking and tears in my eyes, I truthfully said, "It was a relationship of nearly ten years, with four of those years married. I can't say the tree caused the divorce, but the tree has touched each and every aspect of my life."

With me in a weakened state, he then snuck in something I didn't expect. He inquired, "Have you dated anyone since the accident?" I didn't know how to react. Neither did I know why this was relevant. My mind replayed the last nine months of recovering in Massachusetts, New York, and Florida without showers, wearing my cage, and in physical and emotional agony. I responded truthfully to his cruel question with a bit of disdain, "No, I have not been dating." Then I excused myself to go to the bathroom and regroup.

Upon returning, the lawyers and stenographer were packing up. We were done. What a relief!

Revisiting the Evil Tree

Feeling tense and rattled after the deposition meeting, my mom and I rushed to the hotel to change clothes and then go revisit the tree.

We rode along Route 9 and exited into the all-too-familiar shady downtown district and passed Dr. Z's office. Near the top of Main Street's hill was the multiple-story, brick building where RB had lived, where I visited, and most important, where all my balls had dropped.

My mom pulled up to our former building with its steps and heavy glass door. From where she parked, I looked up to our former studio window. Those panes of glass were my small window to the world when I was just out of the hospital and unable to walk on my own. I got out of the car full of anxiety, feeling more nervous than during the deposition interview that morning.

We walked together across the same sidewalk and down into the same alley and parking area where I had walked that September day. Five months had passed since we were last at that spot. Five months might not seem like a long time, but it was long enough for a lifetime of major changes. At that time, the evil tree limb had still been there in its entirety, placed beside the two dumpsters and out of the way of cars.

To my surprise and to hers, the tree had been moved. In the corner, we saw a recent pile of woodchips about six feet high. The evil tree had made it to a wood chipper. Oh how *Fargo*! I was delighted to know the tree had finally been shredded. Why hadn't they done it sooner?

Regardless, I felt triumphant, almost wanting to run a victory lap with the *Chariots of Fire* theme playing in the background. Instead, I climbed atop the pile and, in my best nasal *Fargo* accent, I joked, "You betcha! If an evil tree tackles me, it ends up in the wood chippa, don't cha know."

I asked my mom to take a couple of photos to document this moment. From atop the pile, I crouched and smiled proudly as if I had just hiked to the top of Kilimanjaro.

To celebrate this topsy-turvy day, as a finale we walked the Walkway Over the Hudson, my Road to Recovery Bridge. Just as I had done countless times in the cold, windy days of winter bundled from head to toe in a heavy coat, scarves, mittens, boots, and long underwear, I admired the beauty of the hills and river. Oddly enough, on this walk, I could see the similarities of the Hudson River Valley with where I grew up near the tree-lined bluffs cradling the Mississippi River.

Basking in the summer's sun with my mother at my side, I felt a page had been turned. It was the beginning of another chapter.

Epilogue

AFTER NINE MONTHS OF THE MOST PAINFUL, CHALLENGING obstacles I had faced in my life, I understood that on that September afternoon, I had not been at the wrong place at the wrong time; I was at the right place at the right time.

It was a long time coming—this kick in the ass and smack in the face that had become so necessary for me to drastically alter my life.

As Zen masters say, you cannot see your reflection in running water, only in still water. And I certainly couldn't see my reflection juggling everything that I had on my plate. It took a radical halt to all of the distractions for me to see clearly what I wanted, how I needed to change, and who I wanted to become.

I'm not the same person who woke up in St. Francis not knowing what had hit her. Rather, I'm a better version of that person. My priorities have shifted. My health, my relationships with my clan, and my passions for a new career have become paramount. Along the way, I made many mistakes that probably could have been avoided, but society and my own fantasy of the perfect life kept leading me down the wrong path. It was only when I was given *no choice except to slow down* that I took the opportunity to learn the lesson that saved my happiness.

One may think that, after such a test and winning against all odds, I would never forget the lessons. But old habits—and bad habits at that—are hard to break. That's why I started Look Up Day. It reminds us all to, first, slow down and be aware of our surroundings and, second, take each situation and spin it positively.

I share Look Up Day—the twenty-seventh of every month—with you.

So if someday you're rushing to take out the trash, and you look at a text from your boss saying don't bother coming in because you're fired, and you go to the dumpster anyway and notice a bright-pink note from your significant other dumping you, and in a heartbroken rush, you turn, slip, and fall into a pile of dog shit—take heed from the parrot that's squawking on the tree limb high above: "Look up!"

Here's to looking up!